# THE TWENTIETH-CENTURY
# INTERIORS
# SOURCEBOOK

Published in 2013 by Goodman Fiell
An imprint of the Carlton Publishing Group
20 Mortimer Street
London W1T 3JW

www.goodmanbooks.co.uk

A CIP catalogue record for this book is available
from the British Library.

Text © Carlton Publishing Group 2013
Design © Carlton Publishing Group 2013

ISBN 978–1–78313–000–9

Printed in China

# THE TWENTIETH-CENTURY

# INTERIORS SOURCEBOOK

## FROM ART NOUVEAU TO MINIMALISM

Clive Edwards

GOODMAN
FIELL

# Contents

# Introduction

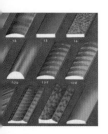

**In this analysis of twentieth-century interior design we take in a wide range of interiors – mainly from the affluent Western industrialized world – from design conception to final consumption, through development, production and mediation. By looking at a varied range of interiors from the decades that make up the century, it is possible to see a complex and interwoven pattern of design solutions to the spaces we use and inhabit. Although the book follows a chronological progression for ease, the complexities and contradictions in twentieth-century interior design are not so straightforward. The meanings of objects, products and spaces change over time. The very term "interior design" has had different connotations over the century.**

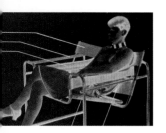

At the beginning of the century, the processes now known as interior design were still mainly in the hands of architects or retailers. At this stage, small developments sowed the seeds for a new profession of interior designers. Initially, decorators, often women, set themselves up as selectors of appropriate materials, finishes and furnishings for households that could afford their services; some of these decorators went on to establish themselves as interior design businesses. Architects also remained interested in interiors, and gradually many practices developed departments for interior work. After the Second World War there were calls for the professionalization of the business with the concomitant demands for education and infrastructure, codes of conduct, and professional bodies to support and promote the business. Interior design by the end of the century referred to a professionally conducted, practice-based process of planning and realization of interior spaces and all the elements within, creating a definition which includes both interior decoration and interior architecture.

However the practice is defined, the twentieth century was witness to some of the most important changes in the nature of interior design that have ever occurred. A number of factors brought about changes that had a great bearing on how people related to the spaces they designed, lived, worked and played in. An investigation of these changes and the factors involved is crucial to understanding how interiors developed and changed over the century. Considering the history of the twentieth-century interior by decade allows us to see how these developments reacted with and upon each other, overlapped or disconnected to create the various and particular visual results we see in this book. The areas of change that influenced twentieth-century interior design can be classified as: social elaboration, cultural issues, techniques and technology, political influences, geographical and media considerations and, most importantly, design issues.

## SOCIAL CHANGES

Societal changes are interconnected, meaning that one change will bring about others. For example, during the twentieth century, these social changes include a negation of discrimination based on race and sex and the subsequent fight for equality; a near universal understanding of the effects on the environment by human activity; the impact of technology on how we live our lives and the effects of an ever-growing population on feeding and housing.

In terms of interiors, these changes have also related to matters of consumption, taste, people's changing hierarchy of needs and the role of psychology and signification within interiors. An understanding of the influence of psychology and the pleasure derived from the making and use of interiors became an important factor in interior design. Interiors have always reflected aspects of society, but as a majority of people in the twentieth century – particularly in the developed world – were able to engage with interiors to a greater extent than ever before, the significance of these factors was clear.

The denial of the domestic by some modern architects was in opposition to a renewed interest from the public in their own living spaces. What is clear is that issues of privacy and space as well as the recognition that the interior is a symbolic expression of self (individual or corporate), have always been of prime importance once necessities have been met. Therefore, an issue central to the discussion of interiors is their role as repositories of ideas and objects, a role that is both physical and emotional. It is also undeniable that there has been a see-sawing between the rational and emotional approaches to the home that has been at the base of many of the arguments and changes in twentieth-century interiors. The shift from rigid distinctions between architecture, design and decoration to something of a synthesis was a result of this process.

## CULTURAL ISSUES

The second factor that influenced interior design is related to cultural identity. Culture is defined here as an amalgam of groups of peoples, their values and beliefs and the objects they produce and consume. Therefore, interiors, like any other designed objects, illustrate the massive changes that occurred during the twentieth century in terms of culture. These changes related to issues around class and status, gender, sexuality, attitudes to disability, changes in family life and composition of household, the increase in people working from home, social conformity and non-conformity, symbolism of the home and its spaces and objects, and the distinctions between the amateur and the professional in terms of decorating and designing. These cultural issues influenced the nature of business and public interiors as much as the domestic did. In addition, the changing role of women in society and the development of feminist histories have altered the way in which the concept of interiors, especially homes, is now considered.

One example of a cultural change that affects interior design is that since 1985, in the wealthier countries, the average number of people co-habiting in a household has been falling. The rate of divorce and the increase in single-person households have

**ABOVE**

*Interior of Stansted Airport, England, by Norman Foster. 1988–91.* The demands of airlines and their passengers require a very particular type of interior design that meets a number of conflicting needs.

altered the nature of the housing market and the design and decoration of interiors. In a broader sense, this has increased demand for buildings and furnishings that affect the economy and the ecology of the planet.

Changes in the way people lived and worked during the century also saw the need for the rapid development of new types of spaces including offices, hotels, retail premises and travel interiors. The new or redeveloped interior spaces reflected these cultural changes. The re-interpretation of building types such as hospitals, civic buildings, museums, restaurants and bars, and even religious structures, related to societal shifts as much as domestic spaces did.

## THE ISSUE OF TASTE

There are also aspects of the domestic interior that have been continuous during the century. These are often based on conventions that are rooted in issues of identity. The making of identity through the interior is subject to the conflict between continuity and change. An individual's lack of control over product choice hindered the development

**LEFT**
*Living room display in Habitat store, Terence Conran, c.1966.*
*The influence of the modern movement in the furniture is offset by the use of decorative accessories.*

of their identity, until shops established the idea that identity could be learned and purchased, so the market appears to give us tools to create our own identity, but with the retailer often taking the role of taste-maker.

For much of the century, the issue of taste was responsible for this confusion. Interior design and decoration was bound by many conventions in the approach to design of any particular spaces, and these were more or less formal – approved, correct, impersonal, prescribed and rigid or regulated taste. Taste-makers represented these conventions through the so-called rules of taste. But many householders strove to make their spaces homely – comfortable, congenial, cosy, familiar, intimate, modest, plain, relaxed, snug, unpretentious or informal. In most cases, they were trying to represent themselves and their perception of their place in society, whilst at the same time locking into accepted tastes and imagery. The creation of an individual home that was both fashionable and personal resulted in an eclectic interior. There was a certain amount of risk in this compared to the certainties of the Modernist era, where it seemed that it was difficult to go wrong if the rules were adhered to. For much of the twentieth century, there was a conflict between the formal, prescribed home ideal, the opposite decorative and symbolic approach, and the real, cosy actuality that many people really aspired to.

The "battle of the styles" that characterized much of the nineteenth century signalled the beginning of a set of changes that reflected the decline of a definite ruling taste for a more individual and eclectic, if not sophisticated, approach to decorating. Having gone through any number of historical and exotic borrowings to create styles during the century, the later years of the nineteenth century were dominated by a number of definable visual approaches. These included the vernacular influence of the Arts and Crafts and Craftsman movements, the artistically inclined Aesthetic and Art Nouveau styles and the classically led Beaux Arts. Overriding all these was an approach best described as eclectic.

These approaches to interior design recognized that there was no one "correct" style, although many supporters of each believed there was. During the twentieth century, the period between 1900 and 1925 saw the beginnings of choice for sections of the population that had previously been unable to engage significantly with interests in homemaking beyond necessity. These changes were brought about by more buyers who were able to afford new furniture due to a rise in disposable income and access to credit facilities and an increase in planned housing programmes which encouraged new furnishing purchases – all of which led to a desire for interiors that reflected differentiation but emulation of particular tastes, which in turn led to greater expectations and greater demand for choice. However, ideas of decorum still controlled this approach, based on established taste and knowledge. Cultural consumption (or taste) is a pattern of social distinction that legitimizes forms of power and control based on economic situations.

The battleground between the various performers and creators of interiors was polarized between the architect and professional designer, whose ideas of interior design were inextricably linked to the architectural shell, and amateur interior decorators and home-makers who preferred to create lifestyle spaces not necessarily related to the building that housed the spaces. This was to develop later into sharp distinctions between the concepts of the total work of art, scientific management and modernity in contrast to matters of self-identity, expression and individuality.

**RIGHT**
*Advertisement for decorative mouldings, France, 1920s. The importance of choice and selection was crucial to the development of individual interior decorations.*

**FAR RIGHT**
*An ensemble of furniture in an interior designed by R. Couraillier, France, 1920s.*

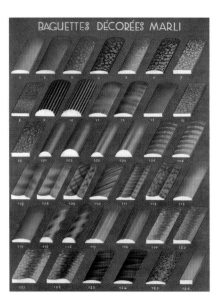

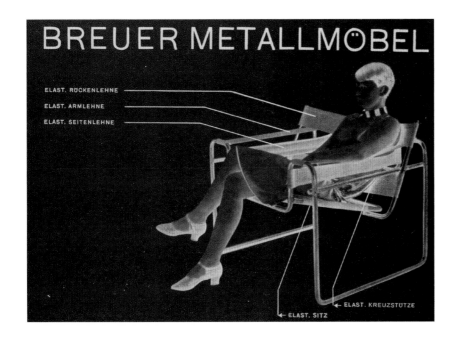

ELAST. RÜCKENLEHNE
ELAST. ARMLEHNE
ELAST. SEITENLEHNE

ELAST. KREUZSTÜTZE
ELAST. SITZ

**LEFT**
*Advertisement designed by Herbert Bayer, Bauhaus, 1927.* The iconic Modernist B3 chair by Marcel Breuer is featured.

## POST-WAR MODERNISM

It is a truism that wars are often social watersheds, but the social and political changes brought about by the end of the First and Second World Wars had far-reaching effects, not least on interior design. One particularly potent movement was Modernity, or Modernism. Modernism in interior design and architecture developed after the turmoil of the First World War partly as a response to political ideas based on a vision of inclusivity, freedom from war and want and a utopian vision of the future. Modernists never conceived their approach as simply another style, rooted as it was in intellectual ideas. There were various national and international aspects of Modernism but they all maintained particular values. These included ideas of a negation of the past, a refutation of the use of applied ornament, the use of the abstract rather than the decorative or figurative and a notion that through design and the use of technology society would be improved and ultimately achieve its utopian goals. Terms such as Modernistic, Avant-garde, Moderne, Streamlined, Contemporary and Minimal are all aspects of or versions of Modernism.

The attempts at establishing Modernist codes that apparently signalled the correct and proper ways of creating homes was clear in Marcel Breuer's 1931 lecture, which implicitly stated that the architect was in charge of the interior as much as the exterior:

> In the ideal (or more properly stated the correct) situation, the interior is no longer an independent unit set in the house, but is constructively tied to the building itself – properly speaking it begins with the floor plan rather than after the completion of the building. Only the ideal situation allows for this organic unity that is the completely furnished new construction.[1]

While Modernism appeared to dominate the interior design scene for many years, it is as well to acknowledge that interiors often reflected people's individuality and taste and high-level needs which is a reminder that there was no such thing as a true ruling taste in the twentieth century. One could even argue that Modernism was another style that stood in stark contrast to the desire for cosy decorative arts, common-sense furnishing, enjoyment of fashion as escapism and a desire for domesticity.

Eclectic approaches based on interpretation or copies of past design works played a persistent part in twentieth-century interiors. All of the period styles, or adaptations of them, provided by decorators or retailers reflected people's desires for some continuity in their interiors. The underlying ethos of particular styles historic styles, such as Renaissance and Regency, may have chimed with specific issues of nostalgia or power play, or they may simply have been reactions to previous styles. Interior fashions have often played a ping-pong game between the classical and romantic, the geometric and organic, the simple and elaborate, the monochrome and colourful and the calm and excited. These may of course also operate simultaneously.

In a rather different scenario, but still indicating a degree of prescription, was this 1980s *Company* magazine article:

> I promise that the following obvious candidates [of bad taste] will have fallen to the axe, hammer or incinerator – replica Victorian telephones, onyx and gilt coffee table…large red brandy glasses with tiny porcelain kitten clinging to the side…cocktail cabinets…spare toilet roll covers…doorbell chiming tunes…crazy paving…[2]

Whilst it's true that *de gustibus non est disputandum* (in matters of taste, there can be no disputes), another agenda influenced interior design during the twentieth century. This was the rise of the conservation and sustainability movements, whereby rehabilitation and adaptation of buildings and spaces was developed. Conservation is generally taken to mean conserving an existing space or building in its current form, however that may be, at the very least to make it safe but with minimal intrusion. The next level is preservation, which also maintains a minimally invasive ethos but may update systems and buildings to current quality standards, if appropriate. Adaption or the reuse of a building and its spaces, sometimes called adaptive reuse or remodelling, goes further in its interventions into and onto the building spaces.

## TECHNIQUES AND TECHNOLOGY

The changes surrounding techniques and technology were a third influence on interior design. The twentieth century undoubtedly saw more innovation and inventions than any previous era. Technological development and research, sponsored by both businesses and governments, provided products that we now take for granted, including communication devices such as radios, televisions, the Internet, computers

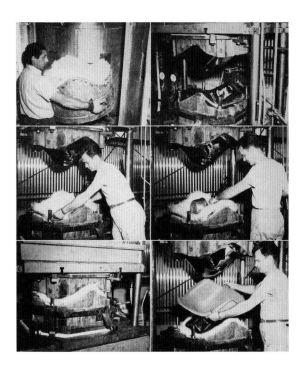

and mobile phones, travel using cars and airliners, domestic inventions such as the humble light bulb, microwaves and frozen foods and many more developments relating to materials, functions, and processes that affect not only the building and services but also issues around living arrangements and comfort. These advances mean that many interiors of the late twentieth century bore little relationship to those of the early part of the century in these terms. The rise of synthetic fibres, plastics, new applications for metals, development of wooden board materials and so on, as well as developments in digital applications and the growth of appliances, meant that a 1990s interior would have been akin to science fiction to an early twentieth-century viewer.

The history of technology and its effect on interior design is an important part of the wider history of "things'" and their uses. Technologies' success is partly due to the physical realities they impart, but just as important to success are the strategies employed by those involved in the development, marketing and use of particular technologies. Technology is beneficial when it connects with the expectations, needs and ideas of those who interact with it and consume it. One of the key breakthroughs for interiors in this sense is the way in which new technologies – wood products, metal tubing, foam cushions, various fibres etc. – made a range of furnishings, once found only in elite households, affordable and convenient for the majority. The choice and range of materials available to furniture makers in the twentieth century was extremely wide. The continued development of metal, plastics and wood-based products was an essential complement to the traditional materials still in use.

The technical changes in upholstery, for example, are related to both internal structure and external coverings. At the beginning of the century, the spiral compression spring was supreme, but in the 1930s, upholsterers introduced spiral tension springs into Germany and England. This released the designer from having to create a deep section to a chair to accommodate the spiral springs: he could produce a more elegant easy chair while retaining the benefits of metal springing. In 1929, Dunlop patented the development of latex-rubber cushioning. When made up into upholstery, this became an ideal partner to the tension-sprung chair. Post-war developments included the four-point suspension (a one-piece rubber platform) and the introduction of rubber webbing by Pirelli. Both of these processes hastened the demise of the traditional spring until the introduction of serpentine metal springs, which enabled manufacturers to produce a traditional-looking upholstery range without the cost of a fully sprung interior. Plastics also earned a place in post-war upholstery with the introduction of polyether and polyester foams for cushions and padding. Developments continued with substitutes for most traditional materials, for example manmade fibrefill in place of cotton-fibre wrap. Manufacturers also used plastics in the construction of chairs, through the development of polystyrene shells that created an extremely lightweight frame. The use of PVC-coated fabrics as substitutes for leather has revolutionized external coverings.

In addition, these new materials were used to produce imitations of traditional furnishings that represented high status on the one hand, while on the other, they also allowed for new designs expressing a modern taste. Besides affordability and symbolism, these products also answered new criteria for high style, cost-consciousness, easy care and home hygiene. Many advances in technology were responsible for developing the markets for individual home makeovers, decorations and DIY, especially in the second half of the century. Whilst acknowledging that consumer choices may, superficially, be based on design and aesthetics, they are but facets of a selection decision. As has been shown, economic, political and social features also play a part in the choice process. All affect the way interiors look and how people design, buy, sell and use them.

## POLITICAL INFLUENCES

The fourth factor influencing interior design in the twentieth century relates to political changes that promoted migration, development of service sector, changes in education, home ownership and consumption, as well as issues around housing and town planning, education and more recently the environment and sustainability. Overall, the economic growth that generally ensured a seemingly ever-growing ability to indulge ourselves in the creation and use of interiors that reflected our lifestyles was part of this process. In addition, growing demand, intensifying production methods, revised distribution systems, increasing social mobility and a growing individualism all led to consumer acquisitiveness, fuelled by the forces of retailing, fashion and advertising.

The engines of a growing population combined with longer life expectancy and smaller and more diverse habitation arrangements increased economic activity and a willingness to buy and use goods beyond simple function, created a pool of greater

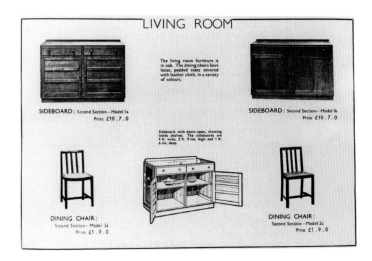

spending power and demand. This meant that more and more people were in a position to acquire new goods. Combined with these factors, there was an increase in urban and suburban living, creating a major source of differentiations between social classes and therefore impacting on product choice. Migration and immigration of sectors of the populace also fuelled these changes. These and other factors ensured that many new manufacturing developments, including those in science, technology and machine-production systems, were espoused as part of a great expansion of consumer culture and the satisfaction of its desires.

## GEOGRAPHICAL AND MEDIA INFLUENCES

Globalization, travel and media also had an important influence on the transfer of ideas through the century when increasing foreign travel broadened tastes and opened horizons. Although it is clear that the West exported many ideas of living practices to other areas in the world, the traffic was not all one way, and Western designers adapted and adopted a number of designs, concepts and images from other regions. The trend towards a fully global economy ensured that by the latter part of the century there was a wide crossover in most aspects of interior design, not least in the products and concepts used.

One particular trend, established in the late nineteenth century, was the publication of advice books and journals that told consumers how to buy and set up interiors. To ensure compliance, commentators and reformers usually peppered their advice with imperatives like "should" and "ought", often with the implicit intention of demonstrating that the home was the most important social institution, meaning any deviation from the norm was anti-social. The great number of journals and books published to help the homeowner "get it right" continued to have a wide-ranging impact on home design. Other external factors were at work to try and influence (and therefore change) consumer habits. Advertising, retail stores, national and international exhibitions and similar sites of persuasion ensured that homemakers maintained ideas and ideals, as these outlets told people what was new and what they wanted.

Another continuation from the nineteenth century was the use of guidelines for the decoration of particular rooms. There was a consistency and continuity of styles that critics deemed appropriate to the various rooms within the house across the social scale. The selection of high-style objects and designs was progressively simplified as they descended the social scale, so that the image of the style remained identifiable, even if only symbolically. For example, in the first half of the century, commentators invariably recommended that English dining rooms be furnished with oak, whilst the main bedroom and the hall also had oak as a preferred furniture finish. It was only in the living or drawing room that the choice was between mahogany, the most favoured, and walnut.

Edith Wharton and Ogden Codman's *The Decoration of Houses* in 1897 was a milestone in interior design publishing. The book's advocation of "house decoration as a branch of architecture" and not as "superficial application of ornament totally independent of structure" was a major change. The authors rejected Victorian tastes as being overbearing, uncomfortable and often unusable. They were concerned that superficial decorative schemes neglected issues such as space planning and the architectural shell to the detriment of the rooms and their users. This seminal work encouraged owners to have rooms created on basic design principles such as symmetry, proportion, balance and, above all, simplicity.

The impact of published media was also crucial in developing twentieth-century interior design. There was a proliferation of magazines promoting anything to do with interiors all through the century, whether they were women's journals, glossy coffee table magazines or trade journals, the verbal and visual aspects of interior design practice were being disseminated to a wider and wider audience. A range of academic interests in many aspects of the interior grew in the latter part of the century, so that a field of enquiry once seen as frivolous became respectable. The arrival of other media including the cinema and later television further encouraged the public as they were continually exposed to new ideas about how to decorate and design. Whether it was luxury hotels or simple DIY, there was to be no escaping the pervasiveness of the interior during the twentieth century.

## DESIGN ISSUES

The final aspect concerns the real and concrete substance of interior designs: concepts, aesthetics, styles, layouts and colour schemes. This book conveniently shows the changes by decade, while also demonstrating that this was not a linear development but rather a set of choices available at any one time. In other words, alongside new conceptual approaches, traditional tastes remained, and in some cases influenced design ideas. Although fashion has always influenced interiors to some degree, in the twentieth century this was ever more apparent. In addition, interior design remained a feature of the work of architects as well as the function of the nascent "interior designer".

Interiors are a major element of material culture and therefore are much more than

**LEFT**
*Roman Pool, Hearst Castle, San Simeon, California, by Julia Morgan, 1927–34.* The bath is modelled on a Roman original in this eclectic 165 room building built for William Randolph Hearst.

simply spaces to act in. The crucial point is that interiors are part of an interactive process between people and things. This interaction is demonstrated by the role of interiors as signs of status and identity; as expressions of aesthetic value; as components of ritual; as vehicles of meaning; as indicators of lifestyle and identity and finally as a focus of discourse. Lifestyles are the basis on which consumers decide on ways to satisfy needs by reference to a range of influences. Issues such as culture and its values, demographics, social status, the role of reference groups, the nature of the household and the individual's own characteristics and perceptions, all come under the umbrella of "lifestyle". In conjunction with this is the nature of the solutions that consumers apply to their needs.

During the twentieth century, the developments that all but expunged the idea of the domestic from Modernist culture actually allowed it to flourish at a popular level of consumption. In broad terms, there were two divisions of change during the century. Initially there were the modernizing and infrastructural improvements led by architects and designers, often with a social agenda: i.e., Modernism. The conventions of architectural Modernism included the formal, approved, correct, impersonal, prescribed, universal, though often alien, ideals that many people received with ambivalence during the period 1920–70.

The second division of change occurred where any consensus appeared to break down, where people enjoyed individuality, and where space was fragmented and personalized in a Postmodern fashion. Actual practices also reflected societal changes from the Modernist ideals of hierarchy and symmetry, based on inherent values and truths, to the Postmodern situation that encouraged eclecticism and valued relativity. Whilst the Modernist agenda for change was based on standardization and efficiency – a common set of principles upon which to design and build homes – the Postmodernists argued for change based on the needs and desires of the individual, and an emphasis on difference. This contrast between the prescribed ideal, established view of conventions (taste) and the real or potential individual self-expression has been the basis for much conflict over the century.

We can also divide interior design in the twentieth century into the residential and the commercial. Residential design refers to the design of the interior of private residences. Some of the seminal buildings of the twentieth century have been homes where the architect has completely designed both the shell and the interior. In other cases, and more often, the interior designer worked on the remodelling of an existing structure.

Commercial design encompassed a wide range of sub-specialities. These included retail premises, malls and shopping centres, department stores, speciality stores, visual merchandizing and showrooms. The twentieth century also saw a major growth in corporate office design for any kind of business, working in parallel with an understanding of the importance of corporate identity. The development of healthcare facilities, in conjunction with changes in medicine and lifestyles, meant that a completely new approach to the design of hospitals, assisted living facilities, medical offices, dentist offices, psychiatric facilities, laboratories and specialist medical provision came about . The enormous increase in demand for hospitality and recreation during the century, which included hotels, motels, resorts, cafés, bars, restaurants, health clubs and spas, created another market for interior design work. Concurrent with developments in twentieth-century architecture, interiors in institutional premises such as government offices, financial institutions, schools and universities and religious facilities were also being reconsidered and remodelled. Even industrial facilities including showrooms, manufacturing and training facilities were re-visited for the new century. Finally, the demand for transport saw work on trains, planes, ocean liners and yachts offer yet more opportunities for interior designers to develop appropriate styles.

Conflict occurs when the dilemma between real self-expression and the dictatorship of style and fashion appears. It is easier to follow the diktats of fashion than to be truly yourself in creating a home. This may explain the spectacular success of ready-made and coordinated furnishing schemes of varying degrees of sophistication, representing the continuity of reliance upon advice or pre-selection; but the difference is that these schemes are often used in conjunction with attempts to personalize one's own space.

The recent past has seen an even greater concentration of attention on domestic furnishings and interiors. The awareness occurs in the form of a plethora of magazines, part-works, radio and television coverage, for example in the introduction of the phenomenon of feng shui, as well as academic interest in the social, political, economic and technological aspects of furniture and home design. Ultimately, individuals make furnishing decisions and the interior always becomes a statement of the owner.

Probably the most important change during the period was the freeing of individuals from the constraints of regulated taste of any complexion and  the embracing of Postmodern eclecticism that challenges the hierarchy of cultural values and allows individuals to express themselves as they think fit. On the other hand, home

*Entrance lobby area, Maggie's
Cancer Care Centre, Ninewells
Hospital, Dundee, Scotland by
Frank Gehry. The aim of these
centres is create a 'domestic'
environment that will help
sufferers manage their fears
in a relaxed environment
of comfort and calmness
rather than a clinical space.*

furnishings still reflect the issues of continuity and historic influences in domestic furnishings. The conflict still exists between the idea that people should choose goods for comfort and use value (people as users of things) versus their desire for 'the new' and fashionable (people as consumers of things), which results in a continual interaction in the field of interior design. To get the most out of looking at and understanding interiors in this book and elsewhere, we need to be able to read them. This is where an understanding of the language of interiors is invaluable.

## THE LANGUAGE OF INTERIOR DESIGN

Interior design language has both principles and elements. The principles include proportion and scale, rhythm and balance, contrast and unity. The concept of the ideal shape based on the correct use of proportion and scale has been a very long-standing one in design. For example, specific proportions identified as the Golden Section, or the Fibonacci series, explain these ideas. Many twentieth-century Modernist interior designers and architects embraced the ideals of Euclidean geometry. The work of architects like Mies van der Rohe and Le Corbusier recognized the elemental importance of proportion. Indeed Le Corbusier devised his own version called the Modulor. In the latter part of the century, encouraged by digitalization, designers used non-Euclidean geometries, for example creating hyperbolic and elliptic effects. Frank Gehry is one of the most famous twentieth-century exponents of this approach.

Scale in interior design relates the various parts to a whole and refers to the relative size relationship between elements of a whole. Although designers often link scale to human sizes and proportions, they may increase it for particular dramatic effects. A simple example might be a double-height room such as Pierre Chareau's Maison de Verre in Paris; more dramatic might be the tall atriums found in later twentieth-century hotels.

The creation of a sense of equilibrium in an interior is important as it creates a feeling of wellbeing. Designers create this harmony by considering balance built around an axis. The idea that a combination of vertical lines that are energizing and horizontal lines that are relaxing can also create harmony. Often wrongly equated with symmetry, balance may simply be a pleasing visual arrangement or a more formal matching of elements on either side of an axis.

Another element in the language that can help to evaluate interiors is the issue of rhythm and reiteration. This element provides some consistency to an interior through the addition or division of elements, which are often decorative. Repetition of the same

**RIGHT**

*A representation of Le Corbusier's modular system that he developed between 1943–8. The system of measurements was based on a human body with outstretched arms and was used for a number of his buildings including the Unité d'Habitation in Marseilles.*

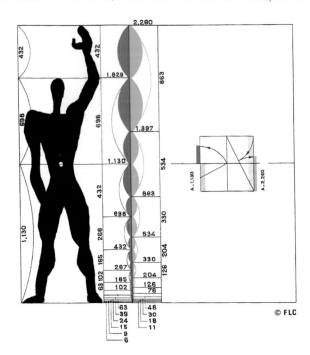

© FLC

motif in different materials, scales and colours can have this effect. Designers achieve rhythm through progression, alternation or repetition. This can be a simple run of a series of columns, say, or a more complex visual repetition of motifs.

The ideas of contrast and opposition set up interesting compositions that relieve the spaces and provide interest. These counterparts may be positive/negative, light/dark, solid/void, large/small, natural/artificial and so on. Designers use contrast as part of the language of expression within the interior.

The relationship between the separate parts and the whole of a design or scheme relates to unity. Unity gives a sense of completeness to a composition, even if the viewer has to complete it. Many of the Modernist designers worked to the principle of the total work of art that ensured the unity of their design. In extreme cases, this would include the architectural shell, the interiors and accessories and even, in some cases, the clothes the inhabitants were to wear. The designers of some of the most famous interiors of the twentieth century have conceived and built around this premise. The works of Charles Rennie Mackintosh, Frank Lloyd Wright, Mies van der Rohe, Elsie de Wolfe and David Hicks all demonstrate this approach. In many other examples, designers create the concept of

**RIGHT**

*Royalton Hotel New York, by Philippe Starck, 1988.* The long lobby space, with custom-made carpet also featured a mahogany-panelled wall. The unusual shiny horn-shaped light fixtures add an amusing dimension to the space.

**BELOW**

*Casablanca sideboard, by Ettore Sottsass for Memphis. Italy, 1981.* The unusual shape and embellishment of this piece were typical of the Memphis group's attitude of irreverence for Modernist concepts of purity in design. The use of plastic laminates reflected the popular culture of the 1950s.

unity with colour, pattern and shape, which are the elements of an interior.

Having established the main language principles relating to interior design, we can now consider the elements associated with them. The elements are the distinctive parts that make a complete whole and include colour, line, shape, texture and pattern. Colour is, of course, one of the key elements of an interior. Colour symbolism and its effect upon users has developed into something of a science during the twentieth century, and many designers have particular takes on how to use colour. Some consider a relationship with nature. In these cases, blue represents sky, green for planting and foliage, and brown the earth and so on. Others see colour as representing states of mind, so yellow is energetic, red is exciting, blue is calm. Yet others make distinctions between ancient muted and faded colours as opposed to bright, primary, childlike tints. The particular application of colour (or not) is also a statement. The vast difference between say a Memphis interior of the 1980s and a white Minimalist space of the same period speaks volumes about the intentionality of the designers. Colour is much more than just a statement: it has the ability to influence people's feelings and states of mind to a degree.

Lines are another important element in interior design as they define a shape by creating edges. Lines can take many forms and therefore have a multitude of roles. Lines as defining elements may emphasize active power and support if they are vertical, whilst the horizontal line may define a more restful, relaxed approach. In another case, the diagonal is action orientated. Curved lines may be formal and geometric or free forms such as those lines found in much of the decorative work of the Art Nouveau

**LEFT**
*Interior of the Guggenheim Museum, New York, by Frank Lloyd Wright, 1959.* The famous inverted ziggurat design also has reference to shell shapes in the spiral internal arrangement of the gallery.

period. Interiors by Gaudí, Guimard and Horta all demonstrate this use of line as a sign of freedom from restraint. Lines, through their particular delineations, can show movement, suggest rhythm, or even signify emotions. The psychological effects of line create apparent changes in proportion and have an impact on the perception of space, so that horizontal lines appear to flatten, while vertical lines tend to heighten spaces. Frank Lloyd Wright's work often makes use of strong vertical and horizontal lines in both the building structure and its interior. Likewise, the works of Josef Hoffmann emphasize the geometry of the line and the square.

The next element is form. This can describe the defining shape of the whole idea, both internally and externally, and may be natural or fabricated. Form identifies spaces as the prescribed idea of what we know to be a particular shape or interior. The simpler contrast between an open-plan space and an enclosed room demonstrates this idea. Form is also partly responsible for identity creation. The 1962 TWA airport terminal by Saarinen and Frank Lloyd Wright's Guggenheim Museum of 1959 are both examples of the use of form to express an idea of shape and internal movement.

Designers also make use of texture, for example to accent an area so that it becomes more dominant than another part. The tactile nature of materials and their textures is especially significant in interior design. If not fully considered, surfaces may often simply reflect the material's texture through fact rather than through deliberate and considered choices that can offer sensory experiences. The physical impressions created by materials through texture will create psychological responses dependent upon hardness, softness, tension and the semiotics of the material. For example, contrasting textures are useful for visual interest in Minimalist spaces. The famous white rooms by Syrie Maugham from the 1930s used textures to differentiate between surfaces.

In interiors, pattern may be intrinsic in the building fabric itself, or surface enrichment will provide it, often helping to create a unified design. For particular styles such as the Arts and Crafts or the Art Deco, pattern was generally an essential part of the interior. The works of Eliel Saarinen and Edgar Wood, among many others, demonstrate this. However, many designers saw applied pattern as an unnecessary addition to an interior. If any pattern was to be used it was often through the materials themselves. For example, Mies van der Rohe's use of marble and onyx for interior walls as well as luxuriously patterned wood veneers added a decorative element without resorting to the historical lexicon or using applied decoration. In another vein entirely, the Postmodernists were eager to raid history and borrow decorative motifs for their interior work. The examples of Memphis are well known but other more discreet examples can be found in many designers' work.

Analysis of these elements in conjunction with the principles above, will allow the viewer to more satisfactorily read an interior whether through an image or in a real space. The final piece of the jigsaw in the understanding of the twentieth-century interior is to consider the context of the spaces. Seeing the broader environment of interiors as part of a system that combines people, design, buildings, the urban

**OPPOSITE**
*The Tugendhat Villa, Brno, Czech Republic, by Mies van der Rohe, 1927–30. This iconic house was one of the first to develop responses to new lifestyles using modern materials in combination with luxurious finishes. The restored interior showing the onyx walls cladding and specially designed furniture.*

landscape and the particular social and cultural milieu of the time will enable us to interpret the interior. An awareness of other features and stimuli that influence an understanding of interiors, such as the social sciences, psychology, behavioural sciences and anthropology, may also enhance and deepen our knowledge and understanding. This book is intended to assist the reader in this journey of discovery.

**FOOTNOTES**
[1] *Wilk, C., Marcel Breuer, Furniture and Interiors, p.184*
[2] *Price, John, AS Media Studies, Nelson Thornes, 2003, p.170*

# 1900–1909

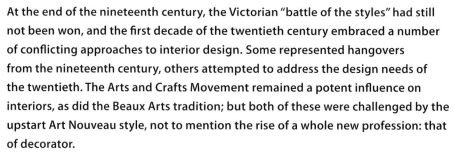

At the end of the nineteenth century, the Victorian "battle of the styles" had still not been won, and the first decade of the twentieth century embraced a number of conflicting approaches to interior design. Some represented hangovers from the nineteenth century, others attempted to address the design needs of the twentieth. The Arts and Crafts Movement remained a potent influence on interiors, as did the Beaux Arts tradition; but both of these were challenged by the upstart Art Nouveau style, not to mention the rise of a whole new profession: that of decorator.

### ARTS AND CRAFTS

The British Arts and Crafts style, based on vernacular models and honestly-crafted objects, continued to thrive in a number of variations and was best shown through the interiors and architecture of designers such as Mackay Hugh Baillie Scott, Charles Annesley Voysey and George Walton. While Baillie Scott's work was frequently colourful and highly patterned, Voysey's was often stark and simple; his own house The Orchard, which was completed in 1899, used plain surfaces, often painted white, alongside simple furniture and vernacular features such as inglenooks. Meanwhile, George Walton designed a series of Eastman Kodak showrooms in London, Glasgow, Brussels, Milan, Vienna and Moscow in an Art Nouveau style that linked with both Scottish decorative motifs and the Arts and Crafts style itself.

It was the Arts and Crafts designers' interest in the past as a model that was important at this time as an influence on a continuing  growing interest in British antiques and vernacular history. For example, the buildings and interiors of the medium-sized country houses designed by Edwin Lutyens represent a particularly English approach to an interpretation of Arts and Crafts that was to remain influential during the first half of the twentieth century. With their half-timbered exteriors, plain plaster walls and bare floorboards inside, Lutyens's houses – such as Deanery Gardens and Homewood – reflected the taste for vernacular that was adapted and diluted in many later semi-detached suburban residences.

The influence of Arts and Crafts beyond England was most keenly felt in America through the work of Gustav Stickley and Greene and Greene. These designers relished skilled woodworking and fine crafts, including stained glass, tiles and textiles used in the true Arts and Crafts tradition. Although clearly influenced by the teachings of William Morris and the vernacular tradition, they thought that the honesty of simple joinery with exposed details represented true American ideals of self-sufficiency and practicality.

Another American influenced by Arts and Crafts ideals was Frank Lloyd Wright. Wright's domestic buildings, often known as prairie houses, were conceived as total works of art, whereby the architect/designer was responsible for all aspects of the building, its interior furnishing and decoration. Although this idea was not new, it was to become a feature of much twentieth century design. Wright's Robie House in Chicago, Dana House in Springfield and Darwin D Martin House in Buffalo all follow this idea of integrated building and interiors.

Back in Europe, the Swedish painter and designer Carl Larsson was promoting his own version of Arts and Crafts, and his homely and domestic images were widely published at the time. They reflected a particular image of Swedish domestic interiors with white painted furniture, simple handcrafted textiles and natural woods. The spread of English Arts and Crafts ideas in house design and furnishing was also aided by Hermann Muthesius's three volume work *The English House*, published in Germany in 1904.

**ABOVE**
*The Gallery in Dana House, Springfield, Illinois, by Frank Lloyd Wright, 1902–04. The architect designed both the furniture and stained glass, demonstrating the concept of the total work of art.*

*Illustration from Das Haus*
*in der Sonne by Carl Larsson,*
*1909. The Swedish interior*
*is influenced by Arts and*
*Crafts ideals and historic*
*Gustavian furniture models.*

## ART NOUVEAU

While Arts and Crafts grew and developed, the vastly different style of Art Nouveau rose meteorically but would not survive the decade.

Art Nouveau was defined by a set of motifs that could be either generally curvilinear or generally rectilinear. The style, which developed and flourished around the period 1880–1910, began in Paris and Brussels, but then spread, with many other manifestations, across Europe and North America. In Italy, the influence of London's Liberty & Co department store meant it became known as the *Stile Liberty*; in the United States, it became known as the Tiffany Style; in Catalonia, it was known simply as

*Modernisme*, and in Germany the style was known as *Jugendstil*, a reference to its youth and its rejection of nineteenth-century historicism.

Various sources influenced the movement, including the Arts and Crafts and Rococo Revival styles, though it was as varied as the designers chose to make it. However, it has been grouped into two types: the sinuous organic (France, Belgium, Holland) and the geometric rectilinear (Scotland, Scandinavia, Germany, Austria), with wide variations in each. The style has some recurring themes, the best known being that of nature as an inspiration for abstracted designs based on plant life.

The curvilinear, naturalistic style was particularly espoused by artists such as the Catalan designer and architect Antonio Gaudí, as well as Hector Guimard, Henry Van de Velde and Victor Horta. Gaudí also produced a unique take on the Art Nouveau style that incorporated elements of orientalism, gothic revival and geometry, as well as organic and biomorphic shapes. Like other designers, he had complete control over many of his buildings and interiors, so he was able to realize the concept of a building as a total work of art. Barcelona's Casa Batlló (1904–06) has an instantly recognizable façade, while the interior reveals many more details of Gaudi's unorthodox approach, including biomorphic furniture, woodwork and lighting.

The work of Victor Horta for private houses and for public buildings, such as the Brussels department store L'Innovation and the Grand Bazar in Frankfurt, reflects a more mainstream Art Nouveau style, but with iron and glass integrated into the sinuous forms. Henry Van de Velde was interested in developments in England and was partly responsible for making connections between British and Continental work. His furniture designs and interior projects also reflect his interest in English Arts and Crafts ideals.

In France, the designer Eugène Vallin represented the Nancy school and Vallin's interiors, especially the Masson house, are archetypes of the Art Nouveau style. In Paris, Hector Guimard was one of the most prominent figures of the movement. Guimard's

**LEFT**
*Exterior of the Casa Battló, Barcelona, by Antoni Gaudí, 1904–6.*
*The extraordinary organic shapes are the epitome of one form of art nouveau design practice.*

Castel Béranger is well known, as is his work for the Metro entrances, but perhaps it is Salle Humbert de Romans or Castel Orgeval that best demonstrate his skills in manipulating line and space.

Art Nouveau designers borrowed extensively from different historical or geographical origins. Shapes based on the vernacular designs of the Middle East, the Far East and Africa, for example, were interspersed with the application of motifs from ancient Celtic and Viking art. They also derived imagery from the metaphysical and emotional facets of humanity found in the work of the Symbolist movement.

Art Nouveau truly was an eclectic style. Art Nouveau in Budapest differed from that found in Glasgow, which differed again from that found in Turin. The Paris *Exposition Universelle* of 1900 was a showcase for the style, and two years later the *Esposizione Internazionale d'Arte Decorativa Moderna* of 1902 was held in Turin, Italy. The latter exhibition featured a large number of specially created interiors, including work by the extraordinary Carlo Bugatti.

In the USA, the work of Associated Artists Louis Comfort Tiffany and Candace Wheeler linked Arts and Crafts skills and values to the creation of interiors, while in Scotland, Charles Rennie Mackintosh and the Glasgow School were to have a major influence on European developments – although the rest of the United Kingdom largely ignored that influence. The style associated with Mackintosh began as an elongated and florid version of Art Nouveau, combined with a variety of imagery, which was later developed into the more rectilinear style familiar in his chair designs and interiors. The competition entry drawing by Mackintosh for the dining room of a proposed House for an Art Lover, produced in 1901, illustrates both these approaches. Mackintosh's brief but productive career had a number of highlights that reveal his skill as an interior designer. The daring use of contrasting dark and light colours in his own house, the famous

**BELOW LEFT**
*The Fountain Court, Laurelton Court, Long Island, New York, by Louis Comfort Tiffany, 1902–5.* The interiors demonstrate Tiffany's concept of the conjunction of nature and art which is influenced in part by the Aesthetic taste for exotic and colourful imagery.

**BELOW RIGHT**
*The double height Reception Hall, Laurelton Court, Long Island, New York, by Louis Comfort Tiffany, 1902–5.*

commissions for Miss Cranston's Tea Rooms and his work at Hill House, all demonstrate his skills with white painted furniture and woodwork, dark schemes for other rooms and an overall passion for orderly and crisp interiors.

The importance of the relationship between art, design and contemporary life was the driving force for the Vienna Secession movement – though in their case the concept of the creation of a total work of art as the ideal often meant ignoring the issue of expense. In 1903, the establishment of the art and design guild, the Wiener Werkstätte, ensured a supply of highly crafted and designed objects for their interiors. They developed a design language that related to new approaches to shapes, materials and colours, and a refreshing idea of simplicity in the applied arts. To avoid repeating historic styles, geometric formulation became the basis for designs. Architects and designers worked together to create some seminal interiors: Josef Hoffman's commission for the Purkersdorf Sanatorium in Vienna, for example, demonstrates a minimal and austere aspect, with simple furniture and black and white floors. Otto Wagner's Post Office Savings Bank, also in Vienna, is similar in concept with a large open space enclosed by a glass ceiling and white painted metalwork with simple functional furniture that clearly points to the future. In contrast, though still reflecting the *Werkstätte* ideals, Josef Hoffman's Palais Stoclet near Brussels is a great example of the concept of the total work of art that integrates building, interior, artworks and accessories with a common visual language of rich materials and geometric patterning.

## BEAUX ARTS

The third major stylistic tendency of this decade was based on the nineteenth-century teachings of the École des Beaux Arts. The influence of the school was found in all sorts of buildings and interiors, ranging from opera houses to department stores, hotels to private houses. Particularly strong in America, the style was used successfully by the architectural firm McKim, Mead and White in their work for J Pierrepont Morgan in New York and in the White House in Washington, both of which reflected the formal Neoclassical stylistic vocabulary. This taste was also fashionable in Britain, where Mewès and Davis's Ritz Hotel in London, built in 1906, reflected the Neoclassical tastes and lifestyles of the *Belle Époque*.

## RISE OF THE DECORATORS

While many examples of progressive design for interiors had come from architects, there was a growing group who were to have a major influence on developments in both commercial and private interiors: decorators. The tendency that had begun in the late nineteenth century for commissioning designer/decorators, as opposed to architects, continued. Two influential American women had a considerable impact on the development of the profession of interior design during this decade.

Edith Wharton (1862–1937) was an American novelist, short story writer and designer. In *The Decoration of Houses* (1897) Wharton and her co-author Ogden Codman sought to move away from the apparent design failures of their time to improve interior design and taste. Wharton and Codman offered both theoretical and practical advice about interior design. They contended that room decoration was an important part of architectural practice, with interior architectural elements as important as the exterior of a house. Their book argued that interiors with classical canons of good taste based on French and Italian styles of the eighteenth century were among the most successful. There was an emphasis on simplicity, proportion, fitness and balance, and they explained these ideas in relation to particular rooms. The apparent elements of good taste, developed by Wharton and based on antique models, were to dominate a particular section of the interior design business for many decades.

Elsie de Wolfe (1865–1950) was another American interior decorator, whose first commission was for the Colony Club in New York in 1905. She was also the nominal author of the influential 1913 book *The House in Good Taste*, and a prominent figure in New York, Paris and London society. Her interior design philosophy, based on lightening and opening up spaces and removing clutter, reflected a growing twentieth-century or modern identity. She used light and refreshing colours, while also creating effects through the use of potted palms, Persian rugs, mirrors and *faux* finishes. The architectural establishment frowned upon all this since they considered the links between fashion, feminism and commerce to be frivolous. Nevertheless, de Wolfe developed a trend for a "decorator approach" to interiors that has become the standard.

**LEFT**
*The tea room/palm court at the Ritz Hotel, London, by Mewes and Davis, c.1905.* The neo-classical style reflects the tastes of the Belle époque.

## OTHER DEVELOPMENTS

The American architect Louis Sullivan, well known for the saying "form ever follows function", is often cited as one of the first modernists, mainly for his contribution to skyscraper design. However his interest in decoration of interiors is seen in projects such as the famous Auditorium Building in Chicago and in many smaller commissions, including the National Farmers' Bank in Owatonna, Minnesota. His combination of new technologies, use of Art Nouveau-derived ornament appropriate for new building types and rejection of the Beaux Arts traditions made him an important link between architecture and design styles of the nineteenth and twentieth centuries.

One of the first purpose-designed business environments for specific company use was Frank Lloyd Wright's 1904 design for the Larkin Company Administration Building in Buffalo, New York. This was a successful mail-order soap company and the innovative design included positioning the main services in the corners, allowing the creation of a large atrium in the body of the building. To maintain indoor air quality, the building had one of the first rudimentary air-conditioning systems. The workforce laboured together in the open galleries that surrounded the central top-lit atrium space. Wright's concern for a total design concept which addressed itself to the client's needs meant that he designed custom-made steel office furniture, and one of the first sets of systems furniture and built-in cabinets for office use. It was in this decade that designers were beginning to further address issues about commercial operating efficiency and function.

Another important development in this decade was the initiation in 1907 of the Deutscher Werkbund. It was intended to link architects and industrialists to improve German design competitiveness – Peter Behrens, Josef Hoffmann, Bruno Paul, Richard Riemerschmid, Ludwig Mies Van der Rohe and Henry van de Velde were some of those involved. The breadth of their interests was defined by their motto *Vom Sofakissen zum Städtebau* (from sofa cushions to city planning).

**BELOW RIGHT**
*The Dining room in the Van Eetvelde House, Brussels, by Victor Horta, 1900. The epitome of Art Nouveau, this complete room shows the typical whiplash motif, but also represents the concept of a complete expression of an ideal.*

**BELOW**
*The specially designed metal office desk for the Larkin Building, 1904. These were not only practical and fireproof, they also demonstrated Wright's commitment to the building as a 'total work of art'.*

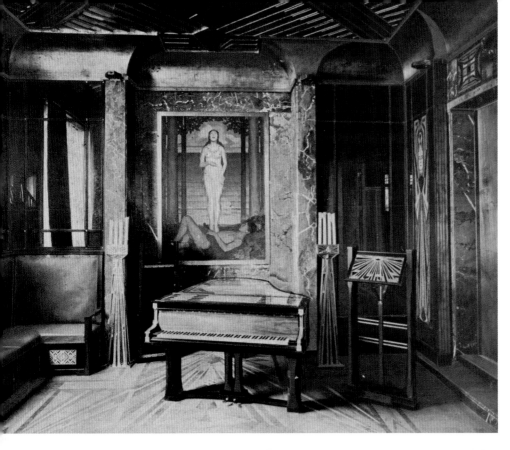

**LEFT**
*The Music Room at Peter Behrens House in Darmstadt , c.1900.*
*The Schiedmayer piano, music stand and two wall mosaics by Villeroy & Boch are evident.*

**LEFT**
*The American Bar or Kärntner Bar in Vienna, by Adolf Loos, 1908.* His choice of materials, quality craftsmanship and particular use of space makes this an iconic interior.

Finally, the work of Adolf Loos was important in moving away from the historicism of the Beaux Arts, and the decoration and pattern of Art Nouveau. In particular, his writings, especially his essay *Ornament and Crime*, encouraged developments which were later to become the Modern Movement of the 1920s onward.

The decade was one of frenetic development in interior design and decoration. New developments challenged the old order on a number of fronts, some of which sowed the seeds for further changes in the following decades. The Beaux Arts tradition lingered on and the principles of the Arts and Crafts continued to be a gentle guiding force, but the search for a new style for the twentieth century had begun in earnest.

**OPPOSITE**
*Design for an interior by Karl Moser, Karlsruhe, c.1900.*

**LEFT**
*Retail drug store interior designed by Josef Hoffmann, c.1900. The stencilled walls and arched woodwork are typical of Art Nouveau styling.*

**LEFT**
*Dining room interior designed by Martin Dülfer, c.1900. The room shows the attraction of Beaux Arts Neoclassicism at this time.*

**ABOVE**
*Design for an interior by Wehling und Ludwig, Dusseldorf, c.1900.*
*This example illustrates the luxurious materials used in interiors.*

**LEFT**
*Design for a theatre interior by*
*Martin Dülfer, c.1900.*

**BELOW**
*Design for a museum interior by*
*Altgelt und Schweitzer, Berlin,*
*c.1900.*

**RIGHT**
*Design for a dining/smoking
room, c.1900.* Decorative
friezes were a feature of
early twentieth-century
taste.

**RIGHT**
*Design for a man's room c.1900.*
This design features typical
Art Nouveau scroll motifs.

**LEFT**
*Design for an interior by Edgar Wood, 1900.* The inglenook, exposed beams and simple matting expose the Arts and Crafts origins.

INTERIEUR
DE LA
SALLE FRAÎCHE

**OPPOSITE**

*Design for an interior by Anton Pössenbacher, c.1900.* The furniture and fittings show the influence of the Arts and Crafts Movement in Germany.

**ABOVE**

*Design for a bathhouse interior by J. Bassompierre, c.1900.*

**OPPOSITE**
*Design for an interior by Hans
Heller, Darmstadt, c.1900.* An
eclectic mix of contempo-
rary tastes.

**ABOVE**
*Design for an interior by Wehling
und Ludwig, 1900.* A mix of
influences from Mackintosh,
Arts and Crafts and even
Beaux Arts traditions.

**OPPOSITE**

*Design for a hall stair and
landing by Edgar Wood, c.1900.*
Wood had a very individual
take on the Arts and Crafts
movement.

**ABOVE**

*Salon by Karl Heckenberger,
1900.* With the white painted
finish, the influence of
Mackintosh is evident here.

**BELOW**
*Design for an interior by Max
Benirschke, c.1900.*

**BELOW**
*Dining room in unknown location, c.1901.* The built-in corner unit and top scroll effects show an Art Nouveau tendency.

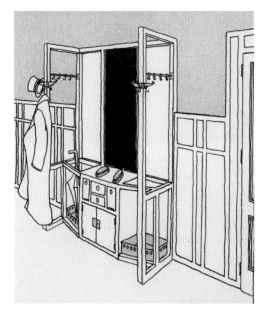

**RIGHT**
*Design for flower stand and hall
furniture, Vienna, c.1901.*

**RIGHT**
*Design for wall cupboard and
seating unit, Vienna, c.1901.*

**LEFT**
*Design for four-poster bed,
Vienna, c.1901.*

**LEFT**
*Design for bookcase, Vienna,
c.1901.*

**ABOVE**
*Design for furniture by Karl
Witzmann, c.1901.* The metal
shoes on the chair legs
and the pattern on the
carpet demonstrate the Art
Nouveau style.

TWENTIETH CENTURY INTERIORS ••• 1900–1909

**ABOVE**
*Design for a music room interior by Valentin Mink, 1903.* An assorted mix of contemporary styles.

**ABOVE**
*Design for a hall by Hermann*
*Billing, Karlsruhe, c.1903.*

**ABOVE**
*Design for a hall/lounge by Edgar
Wood, 1903.* The medieval
romantic strand of Arts and
Crafts is clear here.

**RIGHT**
*Design for an interior by Edgar Wood, 1903.* The decorative panels and solid wood furniture reflect the Arts and Crafts influence.

**BELOW**
*Design for an interior by George Logan, Glasgow, c.1904.* All the elements of the Glasgow Style, including white painted surfaces and rose motifs, abound.

**LEFT**
*The Purkersdorf Sanatorium, seating in the first floor ping-pong room, 1904.*

**OVERLEAF**
*Interior of Casa Batlló, Barcelona, by Antoni Gaudí, 1904.*

**BELOW**
*Austrian Post Office Savings Bank, Vienna, by Otto Wagner, 1906. A functional space that demonstrates the use of modern materials such as aluminium and bent-wood as expressions of Modernity.*

**ABOVE**
*Living room in the Martin House,*
*Buffalo, by Frank Lloyd Wright,*
*1905.*

**ABOVE**
*Fireplace in the Martin House,
Buffalo, by Frank Lloyd Wright,
1905.*

**ABOVE**
*Dining room in private house,*
*Josef Hoffmann, 1906. This*
*dining room demonstrates*
*how Austrian designers*
*adopted the rectilinear in-*
*fluence of Mackintosh in the*
*early years of the century.*

**OPPOSITE**
*Anteroom by Josef Hoffmann,*
*c.1906. This room is most*
*expressive of Hoffmann's*
*newly fashionable elon-*
*gated rectilinear style.*

**ABOVE**
*Magazine illustration of an
exhibition display of the work of
the Kunstgewerbeschule, Vienna,
under Josef Hoffmann, 1906.*

**RIGHT**
*Frau Guttman's study by Karl Wit-
zmann, Vienna, 1906.* Note the
Klimt-like female imagery
on the rear panels.

**LEFT**
*Magazine illustration of a cabinet by Max Benirschke, at the 'Hoffmann Schule', Vienna, 1906.*

**LEFT**
*Magazine illustration of furniture by Max Benirschke, 1906. Journals like these ensured rapid dissemination of design ideas around the world.*

**OPPOSITE**

*A lady's room with a writing desk and chair by Koloman Moser, 1906.* Moser was adept at converting simple geometric shapes into furniture objects.

**LEFT**

*The living room of Herrn Dr S by Josef Hoffmann, Vienna, 1906.* This room exhibits ideas borrowed from the Arts and Crafts Movement in England.

**LEFT**

*Dining room in private house, Adolf Loos, c.1906.* The chairs are modelled on eighteenth-century English examples.

**ABOVE**
*Design for a living space by
Gesellius, Lindgren and Saarinen,
1907.* The surface decoration
indicates the Finnish origins
of the designers.

**ABOVE**

*Design for a living space by Gesellius, Lindgren and Saarinen, 1907.* The surface decoration reveals the Nordic origins of the National Romantic style.

**ABOVE RIGHT**
*The dressing room of Herrn Dr S by Josef Hoffmann, Vienna, 1906. The built-in units reflect a continuing interest in space-saving and hygiene.*

**ABOVE**
*Living room in private house, Adolf Loos, c.1906. The style of the room is eclectic, with a lived-in look rather than making a style statement.*

**RIGHT**
*Dining room in the Robie House, Chicago, by Frank Lloyd Wright, 1908–10.*

**OPPOSITE**
*Children's playroom in architect's own house, Oak Park, Chicago, by Frank Lloyd Wright, c.1900. The mural on the back wall depicts one of Wright's favourite stories, 'The Merchant and the Genie'.*

# 1910-1919

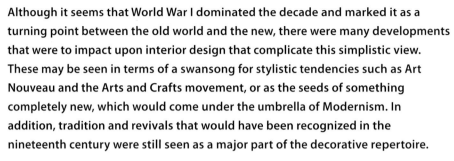

Although it seems that World War I dominated the decade and marked it as a turning point between the old world and the new, there were many developments that were to impact upon interior design that complicate this simplistic view. These may be seen in terms of a swansong for stylistic tendencies such as Art Nouveau and the Arts and Crafts movement, or as the seeds of something completely new, which would come under the umbrella of Modernism. In addition, tradition and revivals that would have been recognized in the nineteenth century were still seen as a major part of the decorative repertoire.

## ART AND DESIGN

Early in the decade there were attempts to link Modern art with design and to enhance the aesthetics of spaces using the artist's way of looking. The art movements that had some influence in this regard included Constructivism, Cubism, Expressionism and Post-Impressionism. Constructivism, espoused by artists such as Vladimir Tatlin, Alexander Rodchenko and El Lissitzky, wanted to address issues that were in every sense real, such as housing and furnishings rather than fine art. Indeed, their ideas were to be influential on the development of the Bauhaus in the next decade.

The Cubist artworks of Picasso and Braque had meanwhile opened up a new way of seeing, which was adopted by architects and designers with varying degrees of success. An early attempt was a maquette for a Maison Cubiste displayed in the 1912 Salon d'Automne by Raymond Duchamp-Villon. This was really a traditional French hotel, but remodelled with Cubist detail. Although there is little in the way of directly Cubist interior design work, it can be argued that it was the basis of much of the Modernist approach to architectural and interior design (see De Stijl and Le Corbusier below). In other works, the play of planes and angles derived from two-dimensional painting was modified to demonstrate a simultaneous experience of inner and outer spaces representing continuity and discontinuity. Cubism also had later influences on Art Deco in the 1920s and 30s.

In Germany, the Expressionists developed an individualistic approach that was opposed to the more analytical and rational work of others. Erich Mendelsohn's Einstein Tower (1919), Bruno Taut's Glass Pavilion (1914) and Hans Poelzig's Grosses Schauspielhaus, Berlin (1919) all demonstrated extravagant forms and fanciful imagery which was often organic, or even spiritual. Expressionism was to be an important influence on the early Bauhaus.

Post-Impressionism had a particular influence on interior design in that bright and indiscriminate colours, as well as geometric forms, were sometimes used to create

**LEFT**
*Entrance to the Maison Cubiste, Exhibited at the Salon d'Automne, Paris, by Raymond Duchamp-Villon, 1912. This detail designed, constructed and sculpted by Duchamp-Villon attempted to demonstrate the integration of art and architecture.*

startling and original effects. Roger Fry, who coined the term Post-Impressionism, established the Omega Workshops Company to produce furniture and interiors in this idiom. Like William Morris, Fry desired the union of the fine and decorative arts in building and design. The venture was rather amateurish, although the firm did publicize their work at the London Ideal Home Exhibition of 1913. In 1916–7 the artists Vanessa Bell and Duncan Grant decorated their farmhouse, Charleston, in Sussex, in the spirit of the Omega Workshops, with most surfaces covered with patterns and artwork. The fashion reached others too: in 1913–14, the "lady-decorator" Lady Sackville designed a room where the walls were emerald green, the woodwork sapphire blue and the ceiling apricot. Yellow and blue curtains completed the ensemble.

**RIGHT**

*The interior of the Glass Pavilion by Bruno Taut, Cologne Deutscher Werkbund Exhibition 1914.*

*Prisms reflecting sunlight were heightened by the reflections of the pool and water cascade on the lower level, all making connections to human emotions.*

**LEFT**
*The Grosses Schauspeilhaus,
Berlin, by Hans Poelzig, 1919.* An
amazing example of Ger-
man Expressionist design
applied to the theatre.
The stalactite effects were
enhanced by a bold red
colour scheme.

## CONTINUING TRADITIONS

Around the world, tradition continued to be combined with innovation. In Scandinavia, the Nordic Romantic style evolved, with a reference to Arts and Crafts that would eventually blossom as Scandinavian Modern. During this decade the interior paintings of the Swedish artist Carl Larsson were widely publicized: mixing Nordic tradition with a light Arts and Crafts touch and a smattering of Gustavian imagery, his work offered an enduring image of the comfortable and easily lived-in home. His use of white paint, which reflected his call for light to be let into houses, chimes with Mackintosh's use of white in bedrooms, as well as other unpretentious interiors, in a loose Arts and Crafts style. More extravagant Nordic imagery was used in some Norwegian interiors by the landscape painter-turned-designer Gerhard Munthe; in the latter part of the decade, designers such as Gunnar Asplund and Carl Malmsten continued to develop a simple, unornamented and neutrally-coloured interior style, based loosely upon interpretations of a Swedish vernacular. Simple furnishings and plain timbers set a precedent that remains with us to this day.

In England the Arts and Crafts tradition lingered, as did Beaux Arts classicism and varieties of revivalism. A fine example of the tradition of woodworking and craftsmanship is Ernest Gimson's Library at Bedales School, built in 1919. Compared to Mackintosh's Glasgow School of Art Library of 1909, it stands as an acknowledgment of the past, while the Mackintosh space looks firmly to the future. But most English interiors made reference to various historic styles during the decade: whether it was Mewès & Davis's Pompeian design for the swimming baths in the Royal Automobile Club in London (1911), or a simple version of a Georgian dining room for a small house, tradition was the norm.

In 1915 an attempt was made to raise the standard of design for the twentieth century through the founding of the Design and Industries Association. Urged on by developments in manufacturing in Germany, and acknowledging the importance of the machine as opposed to handcraft, the DIA proclaimed: "We ought to obtain far greater results from our own originality and initiative than we have done in the past. We must learn to see the value of our own ideas before they are reflected back on us from the Continent."

Although his most important work was behind him, Charles Rennie Mackintosh completed an important interior design commission at a small house in Derngate, Northampton, during 1916–7. There was a change in Mackintosh's style, brought about both by the influence of European designers and by his client Basset Lowke's connections. The colour scheme of the hall was black, with black and white squares, and a frieze of blue, green, purple, yellow and grey triangles. A little later, in 1919, he was recalled to design the guest bedroom, which had as its focus black and white and ultramarine blue stripes, reflecting his debt to the Vienna Secession.

## STYLE DE LUXE

In France, the latest fashions in interior design were associated with the exotic as much as with the decorative. Art Deco plainly had its roots in this period, only to be interrupted by the war. Cubism had kindled an interest in non-Western imagery, and there was still an appetite for oriental and Levantine-influenced designs. The exotic costumes and dances of Léon Bakst and the Diaghilev Ballet Russes, as well as the rising status of *haute couture* and its associated designers, were also influential on interiors at the time. These were often linked with the palette of Post-Impressionist artists.

One of the most famous designers of this period was Paul Poiret. Once a fashion designer, in 1912 Poiret established his decorating business, Atelier Martine, which produced objects and complete interiors in the alluring idiom of Art Deco. A few years later two artists with an interest in decorative arts, Louis Süe and André Mare, formed a partnership and in 1919 established *la Compagnie des Arts Français*: they were partly responsible for setting the groundwork for the style that became Art Deco. Their work was inspired by examples from French eighteenth-century originals, but they put their own spin on the designs using exotic materials and decorative finishes. There were many practitioners of the Art Deco style, and an exceptional example is the early work of Eileen Gray, particularly in the decorating of the Mathieu-Levy apartment in Paris during 1918–19: it demonstrates an interest in the exotic, yet also shows evidence of a more simplified approach that was later to become severely Modernist.

## THE USA

Developments in interiors in the United States during the decade were eclectic. There was a continuing interest in the regional legacy of parts of the country, for example California and Spain, as well as its Colonial and New England heritage. There was also some interest in contemporary European design works, but, for many aspiring decorators, French and English models from the seventeenth and eighteenth centuries were the exemplars. Gothic was even favoured in some cases, such as Cass Gilbert's lobbies and public rooms in the Woolworth Building in New York, 1913, although even this was interspersed with Byzantine detailing and decoration among the Gothic gargoyles and grilles.

Eclectic design sources are also evident on the West Coast. In 1918, Frances Elkins furnished her adobe building, Casa Amesti in Monterey, in a Spanish colonial revival style but with a heterogeneous mix of English, French and Chinese furnishings that led to her recruitment as designer for a number of the region's homes. On the other hand, Irving Gill's Dodge House in Los Angeles, 1916, demonstrates a rare integrated approach based on minimalism and purity of layout: something he probably learnt from his time with Louis Sullivan.

**RIGHT AND BELOW RIGHT**
*Living room and first floor land-
ing of the Walter Dodge House,
Hollywood, 1914-16, by Irving
Gill.* This house had an early
mix of mission style exterior
and modernist interior.
The built-in storage and
the simple balustrade are
noteworthy.

The importance of the interior decorator as a professional was beginning to be noticed. The influence of Edith Wharton and Elsie de Wolfe has already been mentioned; Elsie continued to develop her career with an important commission for the private rooms of the Frick House in New York in 1913. But it was the society decorator Sir Charles Allom who was responsible for the public rooms in the building. A little later, in 1917, Rose Cumming opened her shop in New York, where she offered period elements without any particular historic reference, along with the use of forceful colours and interesting objects.

These women were competition for established interior decorating houses such as Jansen, Alavoine, Jallot, Little and Brown, White Allom and Lenygon and Morant. In addition, the influential Joseph Duveen and his contemporaries sold furniture, artworks and accessories for the grandest of grand interiors. Apart from architectural and decorating firms that existed in most major capital cities, the interior design business was further developed by the introduction of decorating studios in department stores. During 1913, Nancy McClelland set up a decorating salon in Wanamaker's New York store called Au Quatrième; at the same time in Paris, René Guilleré set up the Primavera studio in the department store Printemps. The furnishing departments of many other less prestigious stores offered a full interior decoration service.

During this decade Frank Lloyd Wright was one of the major pioneers of modern architecture and design in North America. He welcomed new technologies, materials and engineering systems, but linked these to a sensitive understanding of their relation to people. This emotional appeal, along with sensitivity to surroundings, made his work harmonius. He was very much of the view that the spaces within a building were the essence of architecture, and he was keen to design the total building, including interiors. Wright's own house and studio, Taliesin, built in Wisconsin in 1911, represented many of his ideals. In contrast his work for the Imperial Hotel in Tokyo, from 1915, confirmed his interest in Japanese design, which when combined with modern engineering made a quake-proof building. This concept of the total work of art has been a source of contention between architects and interior designers, including Wright, who was also a designer of furniture, furnishings and equipment.

## MODERNISM

In terms of interiors, Modernism encompassed a number of tendencies that surfaced in the decade 1910–20. These included the gradual professionalization of the business of interior design; the addressing of issues of urbanization; engagement with new technology and new materials; a consciousness of living in the present; an understanding of the nature of mass markets, media and patterns of consumption and an engagement with the new at the expense of tradition. To achieve the housing improvements and hygiene goals of the Modernist agenda, the benefits of standardization and technology were extolled. Achieving social goals through simplicity in design via the universal was seemingly more important than any individual demands. Like many Modernist manifestos, this plan went against the grain of self-expression, and ignored the relationship of individuals to their spaces and their desire for pattern and decoration in interiors.

It is interesting to see how Frank Lloyd Wright influenced European Modernism. His essay entitled "The Art and Craft of the Machine" (1911), as well as the publication of his works in Berlin by Wasmuth, were influential on the Dutch, particularly those who were to be involved in the *De Stijl* group. In Rob Van't Hoff's Villa Henny in Huis ter Heide near Utrecht, 1916, the influence of Wright is clear in both the exterior and the open-plan interior, and Van't Hoff even designed furniture for the rooms based on Wrightian examples. The open plan interior was a major breakthrough, partly brought about by new building technologies but mainly as a result of Wright's room planning. The *De Stijl* designers saw interiors as surfaces that linked objects and buildings seamlessly. Again, we have a reference to the concept of the total work of art.

In Germany, developments in architecture were to establish the framework for a new approach to interiors. Walter Gropius's Fagus Factory in Alfeld, for example, 1911, was one of the first to use glass as a curtain wall, with interiors full of natural light and spaces dedicated to functions. Germany had, early on in the century, developed links between art, design and large-scale production. The Deutscher Werkbund was founded in 1907 and annual exhibitions and yearbooks published between 1912 and 1915 showed how products for the interior were developing. The important Deutscher Werkbund Ausstellung of 1914, held in Cologne, was a showcase for these new ideas through model buildings. Ideas emanating from this arena were to be influential on the later Bauhaus, founded in 1919. However, it must be remembered that these avant-garde designs were just that, and many German interiors were designed using revival styles such as New Classical, Biedermeier and even Baroque.

Apart from the influence of artistic movements on the modern interior, there were other important factors in play. The continuing impact of technology in the wider world. but especially developments in interior materials including plywoods, wall boards and early plastics, all heralded a decade of change and improvement. In addition, the organization of factories and matters to do with efficiency were to have an impact on interior design planning, especially in the kitchen where the ideas of F. W. Taylor and Christine Fredericks were to be influential.

By the end of the decade, the World War had ended, but conflicts and revolutions continued. Nevertheless, the decade to come (1920–29) was to be one of the most exciting in interior design history as people began to spend more on their homes, architects and designers engaged with urban renewal and interiors became as much a fashion as clothing and accessories.

**ABOVE**

**Imperial Hotel Tokyo, 1916-22, by
Frank Lloyd Wright.** *A view of the
promenade showing Wright's
specially designed furniture and
the decoration of carved Oya
lava blocks.*

**LEFT**
*Deutscher Werkbund Exhibition. Cologne 1914.* The exhibition encouraged the development of the "Neues Bauen" (New Architecture) and the practice of industrial design. Note Bruno Taut's Glass Pavilion on the left.

**BELOW**
*Dining room at the Hotel
Wiesler, Graz, Austria, by Marcel
Kammerer, c.1910.* This room
features an Art Nouveau
scheme complete with a
glass mosaic called 'Spring'
from the workshop of
Leopold Forstner.

**ABOVE**
*The day nursery in the Schiffer villa, Budapest, by József Vágó, c.1910–12.* A light and delicate Art Nouveau treatment is given to a child's space.

**LEFT**
*The night nursery in the Schiffer villa, Budapest, by József Vágó, c.1910–12.*

**ABOVE**

*The billiard room in Café
Heinrichshof,, Vienna, by Otto
Prutscher, 1911.*

TWENTIETH CENTURY INTERIORS ••• 1910-1919

**ABOVE**
*A room in Munich by Karl Bertsch,
1911. The living/dining
room shows signs of an Arts
and Crafts influence in the
chairs and built-in sofa/
cabinet.*

**OPPOSITE**
*Study room in Munich by
Adelbert Niemeyer, c.1911. The
Deutsche Werkstätten furni-
ture manufacturers carried
out the decorations.*

**RIGHT**

*The library in a house in Norfolk by W. C. Stafford, c.1912.* Morris & Co furnished and decorated the room in a conventional neo-Georgian style.

**RIGHT**

*A design for an inglenook by John Ednie, c.1912.* Ednie showed his interior designs with Charles Rennie Mackintosh at Turin in 1902; the influence of Mackintosh is evident in the light fitting and decorative panels.

**BELOW**
*The hall in The Downs, Gerrards Cross, Buckinghamshire, 1912.*
The panelled Tudorbethan-style lounge hall was designed by Arthur Rigg.

**ABOVE**
*The inner hall at 'Undershaw',*
*Guildford, by M. H. Baillie Scott,*
*c.1912. The double-height*
*hall reflects both an Arts*
*and Crafts sensibility and*
*a reference to medieval*
*models.*

**ABOVE**
*The study at 'Undershaw',
Guildford, by M. H. Baillie Scott,
c.1912.* This room is typical
of an Arts and Crafts image
of a yeoman's country
cottage.

**OPPOSITE**
*A bedroom, Germany, by A. von Salzmann, 1912.* The delicate painted furniture and sheer curtains here create a very calm feel, ideal for a bedroom.

**ABOVE**
*Boudoir by Richard Riemerschmid, c.1912.* This delicate room reflects an interpretation of the English Arts and Crafts in Germany.

**LEFT**
*Staircase in Villa Ast, Vienna, By Josef Hoffmann, c.1912.* This advanced-looking hall features a spectacular flooring design typical of Hoffmann's interest in geometric patterns.

**ABOVE**
*Interior designed by Robert Orley,*
*1912.* The mural paintings
were executed by Rudolf
Jettmar.

**OPPOSITE**
*Design for a music room by Franz*
*Schwarz, 1912.* This room designed for a villa in Vienna-
Pötzleinsdorf shows the
influence of Josef Hoffmann
in the grid pattern and wall
divisions.

**RIGHT**
*Dining room by Robert Orley, 1912. The built-in storage and light arrangement are features of note in this room.*

**BELOW**
*The smoking lounge in Café Friedmann, Vienna, 1912. The café culture in Vienna at this time encouraged architects like Theiss & Jaksch to design interesting spaces such as this.*

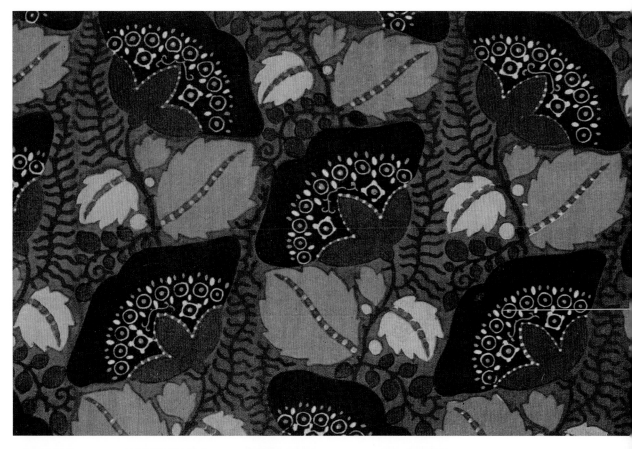

**ABOVE AND LEFT**
*Two designs for printed silks produced by the Wiener Werkstätte, c.1912.*

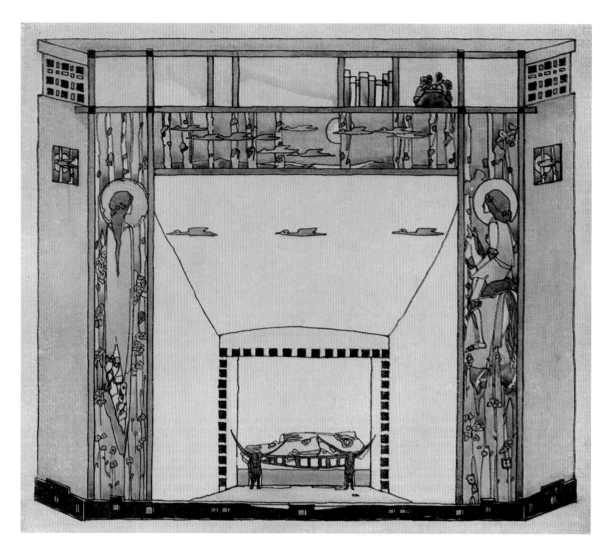

**ABOVE**
*A mantelpiece design by Scot-tish illustrator Jessie M. King,
c.1912. The mantelpiece has
embroidered panels worked
by Elise Prioleau.*

**ABOVE**
*The library in Plas Wernfawr, Harlech, Wales, by George Walton, c.1913.* An interesting interpretation of Art and Crafts concepts with an individualistic touch.

**LEFT**
*A selection of fashionable wicker furniture by Derichs & Sauerteig, c.1912.* The company produced indoor-outdoor furniture when Germany was evolving an important position in wicker furniture-making.

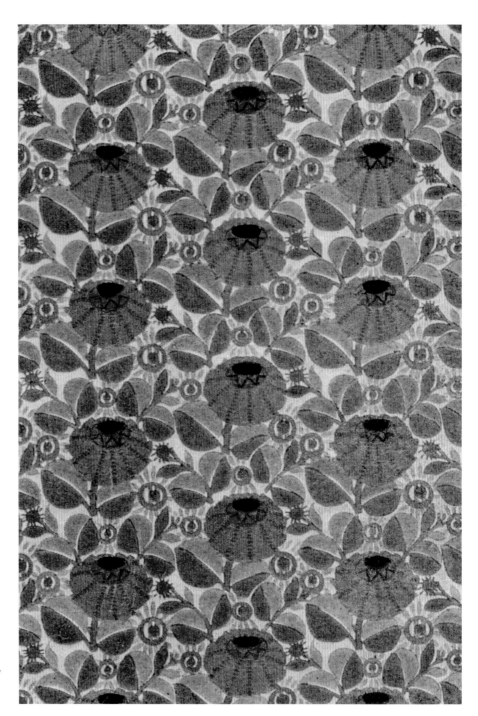

**RIGHT AND OPPOSITE**
*Two wallpaper designs by Eris-*
*mann & Co, c.1912.* These show
the fashionable taste for
small floral repeat motifs.

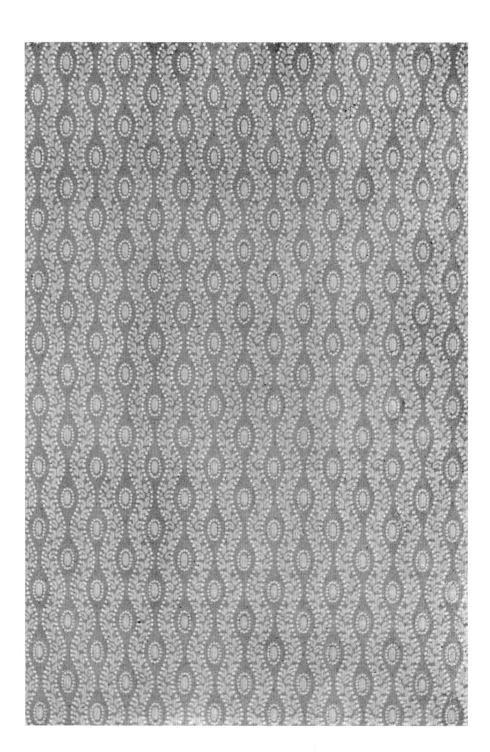

**RIGHT AND OPPOSITE**
*Two wallpaper designs by*
*Erismann & Co, c.1912.*

**ABOVE**
*The entrance hall in a large house in Ulm by Richard Riemerschmid, c.1913*. A much grander hall, with large rugs, fitted stair carpet and lounge area.

**ABOVE**

*The entrance hall in a cottage in Witzenhausen by Richard Riemerschmid, c.1913.* The furnishings reflect a debt to the tradition of the Art and Crafts Movement and were made by the Deutsche Werkstätten in Dresden.

**RIGHT**
*The entrance hall of Haus Huff-*
*man by Hermann Muthesius,*
*c.1914.* Muthesius was an
important architect and an
admirer of English culture
who promoted English interior design in Germany.

**OPPOSITE**
*The breakfast corner in the*
*dining room of Haus Huffman*
*by Hermann Muthesius, c.1914.*
An eclectic interior with a
dramatic ceiling and light
fittings is offset by a simple
curtain arrangement.

**OPPOSITE**

*A ladies' salon decorated in a blue scheme by F. W. Kleukens, c.1914.* This room was part of an exhibition by the Artists' Colony at Darmstadt. Kleukens was a member of the colony at the time.

**LEFT**

*The sales room in clothes shop Des Seidenhauses, Munich, by Gebruder Frank, 1916.* The restrained classicism and elegant simplicity here is a perfect backdrop for a calming retail environment.

**LEFT**

*A woman's bedroom by Josef Hoffmann, Vienna, 1916.* A magnificently elegant, and simple but luxurious bedroom with a four-poster bed and built-in cupboards.

**ABOVE**

*A guest or spare room by*
*Wurzener Teppichfabrik, 1916.*
Fashionable textiles and
rugs relieve the traditional
built-in bed.

**ABOVE**

*The dining room in a house in Vienna by Hartwig Fischel, c.1916*. Ash panelling with a painted frieze above decorates the walls of this dining room.

**OPPOSITE**

*Lady's drawing room in the Haus Schöller, Düren, by Emanuel Von Seidl, 1916.* This grand salon reflects a more leisurely age, with many references to the nineteenth century.

**LEFT**

*The Singerhaus tea and coffee house in Basel by Ernst Eckenstein, 1916.* The unusual arrangement of ground, mezzanine and gallery here create a set of intimate spaces.

# 1920–1929

The decade from 1920 to 1929, also known as the Roaring Twenties, was a period of great change. Despite political upheaval, many people prospered. The impact of these economic changes on homemaking as a sign of new-found stability was particularly noted by The Times newspaper on 28 February 1920: "It may be said without fear of contradiction that beautiful homes make for a contented people."

### BRITAIN

In Britain, the continuity of tradition was evident in much of the decade's interior design. The author and satirist Osbert Lancaster defined the styles prevalent in certain British circles in the 1920s as: Vogue Regency, a gentle and enabling style that would match with most things; Stockbroker Tudor, reflecting an imagined golden age of English life and Curzon Street Baroque, which adapted seventeenth-century designs, many of which soon became clichés. These styles and others were increasingly being supplied by bespoke interior decorators, as well as by a number of large, influential commercial enterprises. The former included the Omega Workshops, where Duncan Grant and Vanessa Bell continued with their decorative schemes for Modernist interiors; Basil Ionides, who was well known for his schemes that were developed around one colour and contemporary architects who developed their own versions of modern schemes, including Sir Bertram Clough Williams-Ellis, Harry Stuart Goodhart-Rendel and Sir Giles Gilbert Scott. The established businesses meanwhile included Lenygon & Morant, Trollope's, White Allom, Keebles and Maison Jansen, all of whom were able to complete full-scale interior decoration and furnishing schemes.

Modernist rationalism, which turned its back on history, was a complete contrast to the establishment position, which was often based on tradition, national identity and continuity. One idea particularly germane to interiors was the aim of imposing order onto apparent chaos or confusion in home design. This "call to order" was based on the idea that less is more, whether in architecture or interior design. The Modernist ideal was one of unity, clarity and function in architecture and interiors. Another prevalent style was the still-developing Art Deco, which was modern without being austere, borrowed from the past but adapted to the new century, and could be found in a wide range of manifestations from the purely commercial to the most exclusive and luxurious.

### ART DECO

These differing approaches were also found in France, where the so-called Art Deco period continued after World War I. Significant works included Armand-Albert Rateau's apartment for the couturier Lanvin in 1928. Rateau is an interesting example of the

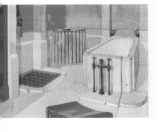

interior decorator-entrepreneur. In 1905, at the age of 23, he was appointed artistic director of the decorating firm Alavoine and Company. In 1919 he established his own business, and by 1929 his workshops employed over two hundred craftsmen. This highly stylized luxury, and France's importance both as a centre of design and as supplier of luxury goods in the Art Deco idiom, was perhaps epitomized by the design and furnishing of the ocean liner Île de France in 1927. So fashionable was this style that in 1931 the Canadian department store Eaton's opened the "Ninth Floor" restaurant in their Montreal branch, almost exactly copying the style of the liner's first-class dining room.

The *Exposition des Arts Décoratifs* held in 1925 was an opportunity for interior designers, decorators and architects to showcase their achievements since the war. Works included Jacques-Émile Ruhlmann's Hôtel du Collectionneur, a dining room by the couturier and interior designer Paul Poiret, and works by André Groult and Paul Iribe. The publication of superb colour plates in works such as *Intérieurs en Couleurs* showed the importance of colour to these designers. At the same time, there was an unashamed use of exotic and rare materials and a high level of skilled craftsmanship which limited access to only a very few clients. Another decorative designer, Jean-Michel Frank, designed an apartment in San Francisco for Templeton Crocker and a salon for the Vicomte de Noailles in Paris, which used straw marquetry, shagreen and vellum: all materials typically associated with Art Deco.

**ABOVE**
*Living room in the Templeton Crocker Residence, San Francisco, 1929, by Jean-Michel Frank.* An article in Vogue (3 August 1929) commented upon "the exotic use of unusual materials. Walls and furniture are of parchment and straw, tables of sharkskin, andirons of rock-crystal, curtains of lacy woven steel like fairy coats of mail…".

**ABOVE**
*Le Corbusier and Pierre
Jeanneret, Pavillon de l'Esprit
Nouveau interior, Paris, 1925.*

In the same exhibition was the contrasting Pavillon de l'Esprit Nouveau by Le Corbusier, Pierre Jeanneret and Charlotte Perriand. This was a statement of unashamed Modernism, which used innovative architectural ideas along with commercially available bentwood furniture and chairs. Here the interior was a machine for living and furniture was simply equipment, as opposed to individual and precious works of art. Le Corbusier's studio had been building and equipping private residences since early in the decade. His La Roche-Jeanneret House in Paris (1923), designed for a Swiss art collector, has all the hallmarks of Modernist architecture: balconies, strip windows, stilts, roof terraces and a moderately plain interior with built-in furniture. By 1929 Le Corbusier had taken his idea of furniture as equipment further, suggesting that pigeon-holes based on a module would suffice for all storage and even act as a wall. Like many other architects before him, Le Corbusier also designed the furniture that he deemed suitable for his interiors. This particular approach to interior furnishings was, however, at odds with human needs and desires – what was suitable in an office environment did not convert to domestic interiors.

Interior work was also key to other French designers who had an outlook that in some ways linked the decorative and the modern. For example, the aristocratic Irish designer Eileen Gray – who had produced some magnificent examples of lacquered work early in her career and who went on to find success in France, built her own house in 1927, Villa E-1027 at Roquebrune Cap Martin. As in her own villa, other interior commissions would include her iconic Bibendum and Transat chairs, as well as rugs, couches, tables and lamps that she had designed herself. Another interesting designer, who stood on the border of Art Deco and Modernism, was Robert Mallet-Stevens. His own house at 12 Rue Mallet-Stevens shows this transition, while his work for the Vicomte de Noailles at Hyères was an early example of the Modernist movement in France. Many components of the interior were supplied by well-known designers and artists: they included furniture by Pierre Chareau, Eileen Gray and Francis Jourdain; stained glass windows by Louis Barillet, and works by many contemporary artists.

**BELOW**
*Eileen Gray's bedroom in her own house E-1027, Roquebrune-Cap-Martin, France, 1926–29. Designed with Jean Badovici.*

**ABOVE RIGHT**

*The Sommerfeld House, Berlin,*
*by Walter Gropius, 1920–22.*
Built in collaboration with
Adolf Meyer and Bauhaus
students, the building
exemplifies their attempts
to create a "unified work
of art".

**RIGHT**

*Exterior of the Schroeder House,*
*Utrecht, by Gerrit Rietveld, 1924.*
The house is a statement of
the principles of the De Stijl
group of artists and architects in the Netherlands in
the 1920s.

## MODERNISM

One of the defining buildings of the Modern Movement was Dutchman Gerrit Rietveld's Schröder House, built in Utrecht in 1924, which clearly shows the integration of the interior, its furnishings and equipment with the building itself. Derived from the ideas of De Stijl, the plan of the first floor is completely open, the walls are movable and much of the furniture is built-in, so allowing the interior spaces to be both contemplated and lived in. The building is defined by the concepts of De Stijl, namely pure abstraction using basic shapes and vertical and horizontal planes along with simple primary colours. De Stijl was also influential on contemporary developments in Germany through Theo van Doesburg's association with the Bauhaus.

**LEFT**
*Staircase in the Café Aubette, Strasbourg, by Theo Van Doesburg and Sophie and Hans Arp, 1928.* The staircase represents ideas of geometry, line and form associated with De Stijl thinking.

In Germany, the developments seen in the previous decade were crystallized in the establishment of the Bauhaus in 1919. One of their first projects was a wooden building, the Sommerfeld House, which was built in 1921. The building's architectural design and interior decoration is linked together in a total concept, reflecting post-war German Expressionism. Walter Gropius founded the Bauhaus school, which espoused one of his main beliefs: that well-designed places and spaces could integrate the individual into society. The Haus am Horn, built for the Bauhaus exhibition during 1923, demonstrated many of the ideals of the new school, including furnishing components specifically designed for each room. The Bauhaus school curriculum put various materials-based craft exercises at the foundation of student work. Formal design and fine art work followed at later stages, but the overarching idea was that architecture was the umbrella art for these other disciplines. The Bauhaus had a deservedly important position in this period of design history, though other developments in Germany were also of interest. The work of Peter Behrens for the I G Farben Building in Frankfurt, 1920–1924, demonstrates the continuing influence of Dutch brickwork design and Expressionism in some very particular spaces.

In the Modernist canon, the interior architecture work of Mies van der Rohe exemplified much of what the movement stood for, and this was often expressed in expensive projects for individual clients. The Tugendhat House for example, built in Brno in 1928 in what is now the Czech Republic, used methods of construction that allowed an open plan, while its use of modern technology for heating and ventilation was groundbreaking. In the interior, lavish materials included onyx-faced walls and unusual tropical timbers. Another example is the German Pavilion built for the Barcelona Exhibition of 1929, which again demonstrates luxury and minimalism. The spirit of the Modern movement, the attempt to bring better design to a wider population, was not really found in these luxury villas.

**RIGHT**
*The German Pavilion, designed by Ludwig Mies van der Rohe for the International Exposition in Barcelona, 1929.* An exercise in the combination of luxury and Minimalism.

More practical was the work of designers such as Margarete Schütte-Lihotzky, and her Frankfurt Kitchen of 1926. These designs were used in social housing, adopting some of the ideas of the home economist Christine Frederick, and workplace planning. In 1927 the important Werkbund-sponsored architectural exhibition of workers' housing, the Weissenhof Siedlung, reflected the new thinking. It comprised twenty-one white-painted buildings that varied only slightly in form, and all had the features that were linked with what would later be known as the International Style. These included basic façades, flat roof terraces, long, horizontal windows and open-plan interiors. Eventually, following closure of the Bauhaus school in the 1930s, Walter Gropius and others took their ideas to England and America, where they become a formidable force in the teaching and practice of art and design.

**ABOVE**
*'Frankfurt Kitchen' from the Professor's Lodgings, Niederrad Hospital, Frankfurt, by Margarete Schütte-Lihotzky, c. 1926.*

## THE USA

In the USA there were four parallel trends that influenced interiors during the period 1920–1929: the growth in interior decoration as a professional business; the arrival of European designers; the influence of Parisian designers and the whole Art Deco and Moderne approach to design and finally the global growth of the interior decoration magazine and book market saw a wider dissemination of ideas across the sector.

The move among interior decorators to become professional businesses had already begun to some degree in the previous decade, but the whole process grew exponentially as demand for status interiors grew. In 1922, Nancy McClelland set up her firm, specializing in recreating historic interiors. As well as establishing a reputation for her interior work, she was a respected lecturer and authority on wallpapers and antiques. McClelland realized the value of training and education for the professionalization of the interior design industry, and to this end she advocated the establishment of standards that included licensing for practitioners. She was the first woman national president of the American Institute of Interior Decorators and published widely in the field of antiques and period homes.

Meanwhile, well-connected designer Dorothy Draper opened her business, and had among her first successes the decoration in Art Deco style of a series of apartment building lobbies. Later in 1929 she was to design the public spaces of the Carlyle Hotel and a Park Avenue apartment block. For this she used black marble with a white contrast for flooring and black woodwork and white walls with limited accents to set off the arrangement. Another doyenne of the business was Eleanor McMillen Brown, who established what she called "the first full-service specialized interior decoration business in America" in 1924. She was to focus on period rooms decorated in an eclectic fashion for wealthy families.

The immigration of European designers to the USA saw the arrival of Rudolf Schindler from Vienna in 1914, and in 1921 he designed the Schindler-Chase House in Hollywood. This residence for two professional couples was built with concrete walls and sliding glass panels, with an open-plan interior intended to be partly communal in its arrangement. The slightly later Lovell Beach House at Newport Beach, California, demonstrates his understanding of spaces and locations that take full advantage of the surroundings. In a different vein, the Finnish architect Eliel Saarinen designed the famous Cranbrook campus at Bloomfield Hills, Michigan, in 1926 as an American equivalent to the Bauhaus. Kem Weber was an early example of the German émigré who helped define modern design in the USA. He arrived in 1915 and stayed to open his own studio in 1924, which designed a wide range of products, interiors and film sets. The Walt Disney studios in Burbank were one of his more famous commissions. These European designers were able to merge the ideals of the Modern movement to great advantage, so that it suited the different attitudes and climate of America; it was perhaps inevitable that modern interior design practice would flourish there in later years.

Art Deco was a natural choice for many American designers as it seemed to fit the new country, which had relatively little in the way of historic practices to fall back upon.

In particular, the public spaces in skyscrapers were perfect places to demonstrate this new taste. The decoration of famous New York buildings such as the Bricken Casino Building, the Chrysler Building, the Empire State Building and the Chanin Building all owe much to the Art Deco style. Ely Jacques Kahn and Jacques Delamarre were experts at devising lobbies and spaces that used luxurious materials, fanciful imagery and elegant colour schemes to create sensational interiors.

**ABOVE**
*The luxurious lobby interior of the Chrysler Building, New York, 1928–30. Featuring marble panelling and exotic wood lift doors.*

## PUBLICATIONS

The importance of books and journals that influenced thinking about decorative practices and allowed ideas and styles to be widely disseminated cannot be overestimated. Frank Alvah Parsons, director of the New York School of Fine and Applied Art, had already written *Interior Decoration: Its Principles and Practice* in 1915, and he followed this with *The Art of Home Furnishings and Decoration* in 1919. In 1922, Edward Stratton Holloway published *The Practical Book of Furnishing the Small House and Apartment*. In 1924, Nancy McClelland issued her work *Historic Wallpapers* and in 1925, she wrote *The Practical Book of Decorative Wall Treatments*. This was followed two years later by another of her works, *The Young Decorator*. In 1921, Louis Süe & André Mare produced a portfolio entitled *Architecture*, followed in 1923 by *Rythme de L'Architecture*, while in 1924 *Intérieurs de Süe et Mare* was published. Paul Frankl, who in 1928 wrote *New Dimensions: The Decorative Arts Today in Words and Pictures*, noted other European influences which included images of work by Dunand, Mallet-Stevens, Poiret, Paul and others. Magazines continued to flourish with the founding of *Pencil Points* (later *Progressive Architecture*) in 1920, *Better Homes and Gardens*, first published in 1922, and *Architectural Digest* which followed in 1925.

The tremendous variety of interior design seen in this decade is witness to the broad nature of the tastes of the time. Whether it was the adaptation of Mayan imagery in Frank Lloyd Wright's Ennis House, the fanciful romantic designs of Hearst Castle in California, the Dadaist interior of Tristan Tzara's house designed by Adolf Loos or the weirdly eclectic Tuschinski Theatre in Amsterdam, it was clear that the variety added up to a truly diverse decade for interior design.

**ABOVE**
*Ennis House, Los Angeles by
Frank Lloyd Wright, 1923–4. The
interior shows his Mayan-
inspired decoration along
with his familiar geometric
glass windows.*

**RIGHT**
*Design for a bedroom by Francis
Jourdain, 1920.*

**BELOW**
*Design for a child's bedroom by
Francis Jourdain, 1920.*

**LEFT**
*Design for a luxury Romano-British bathroom, England, 1924.*

**LEFT**
*Design for a modern functional bathroom, England, 1924.*

**RIGHT**
*Design for a living room by André Groult, 1924.*

**BELOW**
*Design for a deluxe dining room by Pierre Chareau, 1924.*

**LEFT**
Design for a luxurious bathroom
by Pierre Chareau, 1924.

**LEFT**
Design for a bathroom, Pierre
Chareau, c.1920s.

**OPPOSITE**
*Design for a young girl's bedroom by André Groult, 1924.*

**LEFT**
*Design for a hall with interior fountain, Robert Mallet-Stevens, 1924.*

**BELOW**
*Design for a hall/entrance with modern art display by Robert Mallet-Stevens, 1924.*

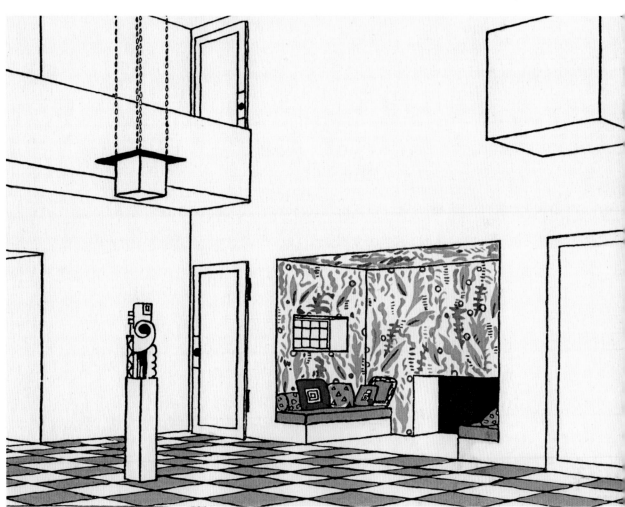

**ABOVE**
*Design for a Modernist living*
*room by Francis Jourdain, 1924.*

**ABOVE**
*Design for a Modernist living
room by Francis Jourdain, 1924.*

**RIGHT**
*Pattern for wallpaper with typical Art Deco furniture by Bucheron.*

**BELOW**
*A living room by Robert Mallet-Stevens, c.1920s.* The unusual centre table and light is noteworthy.

**LEFT**
*A luxuriously appointed study by
Jean Laurent, c.1920s.*

**BELOW**
*Office of Walter Gropius, director
of the Bauhaus, Weimar, 1924.*
*Carpet designed by Gertrud
Arndt.*

**RIGHT**
*Design for a young girl's bedroom by Jacques-Émile Ruhlmann, 1924.*

**BELOW LEFT**
*Design for a luxurious dining room by Jacques-Émile Ruhlmann, 1924.*

**BELOW RIGHT**
*Design for a bedroom with elevated bed by Michel Dufet and Louis Bureau, 1924.*

**OPPOSITE**
*Design for a bedroom with luxury furnishings by Jacques-Émile Ruhlmann,s 1924.*

**RIGHT**
*Apartment with minimal decoration by Djo-Bourgeois, c.1920s.*

**BELOW**
*Design for a modernist 'ensemble' by Georges Djo-Bourgeois, c.1920s.*

**OPPOSITE**
*Dining area in apartment by Djo-Bourgeois, c.1920s.*

**RIGHT**
*Design for a studio space by
Atelier Martine, 1924.*

**OPPOSITE**
*Design for a stairwell with dra-
matic pattern effects by Atelier
Martine, Paris 1924.*

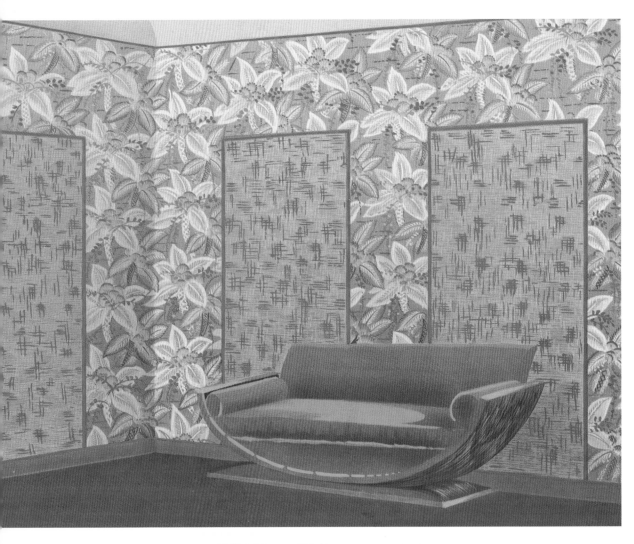

**ABOVE**
*Pattern for wallpaper scheme and sofa, c.1920s.*

**RIGHT**
*Pattern for wallpaper with furnishings, c.1920s.*

**ABOVE**
*Pattern for wallpaper scheme*
*'Doux Rivage', c.1920s.* The motif is repeated in the drapes
and lampshade.

**BELOW**
*Design for a dining room by René Lalique, France, c. 1925.*

**ABOVE**
Design for a studio, Paris, Louis
Süe and André Mare, c.1920s.

**LEFT**
Design for a salon, Paris, Louis
Süe and André Mare, c.1920s.
*Shows an adaptation of
Neoclassical forms.*

**RIGHT**
*Boucher wallpaper showing different borders and panel effects, 1925.*

**BELOW**
*Boucher wallpaper showing various dramatic effects, 1925.*

**OPPOSITE**
*Boucher wallpaper showing various bedroom treatments, 1925.*

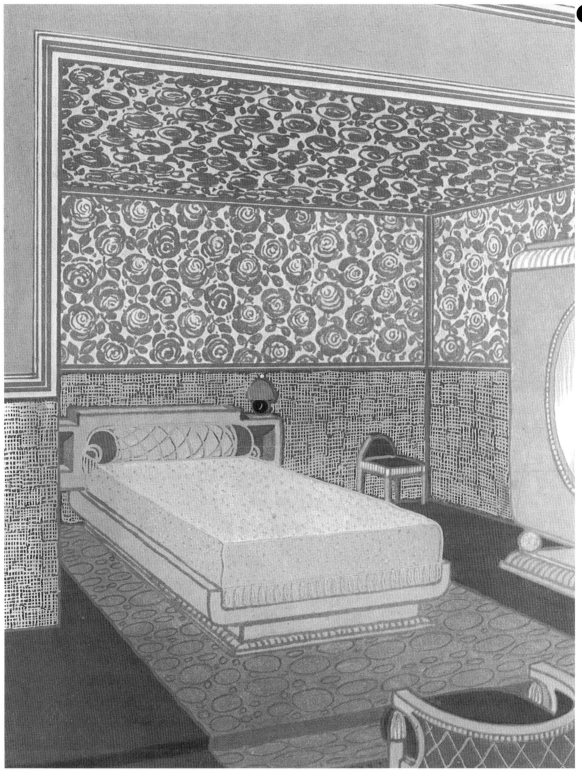

**LEFT**
*Boucher wallpaper designs in typical Art Deco colour scheme, 1925.*

**LEFT**
*Wallpaper design with typical swags and grille (large-scale mesh) effects, c.1920s.*

**RIGHT**
*'Monte Carlo Boudoir' by Eileen Gray, Paris, 1923.* Designed for the Salon des Artistes Décorateurs, French critics condemned it as "a chamber for the daughter of Dr. Caligari in all its horrors," but other Modernists were more sympathetic to her ideas.

**BELOW**
*Room in a private house in the Rue du Docteur Blanche, Paris, by Le Corbusier and Pierre Jeanneret, 1927.*

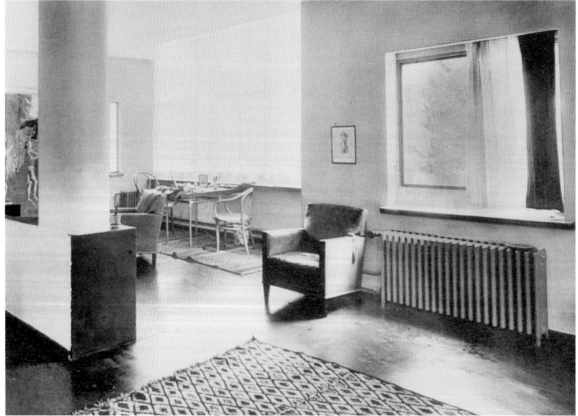

**BELOW**
*An ensemble of furniture designs by Le Corbusier, Charlotte Perriand and Pierre Jeanneret, c. 1928.*

**RIGHT**
*A boudoir in sycamore and lacquer by Léon Jallot, 1928.*

**BELOW**
*A comfortable Parisian living room by Pierre Chareau, 1928. With his famous wedge-shaped nesting tables.*

**LEFT**
*Design for a small bar by Georges Djo-Bourgeois, c.1928–29.*

**LEFT**
*The lobby of the Guardian Bank building, Detroit, by Wirt Rowland, 1928–29. Aztec imagery, often in ceramic tiles, decorates the cathedral-like Art Deco interior.*

**RIGHT**
*Design for a hall by H. Sticht,
Barmen, 1929.*

**BELOW**
*Vestibule of a country house by H.
Becher, Elberfeld, 1929.*

**LEFT**
*Atelier of French printmaker Jean Carlu, Paris, designed by Louis Sognot, 1929.*

**RIGHT**
*Design for a corner of a corridor
by Fr. Kuhn, Vienna, 1929.*

**RIGHT**
*Design for a vestibule by J.
Demetz, Vienna, 1929.*

**BELOW**
*Design for a living space by W.
Gutmann, Frankfurt, 1929.* This
interior shows some influence from Scandinavia.

**ABOVE**
*Dining room by Robert Mallet-Stevens, 1929.* Modernism is demonstrated by the metal furniture and strict geometric layout.

**OPPOSITE**
*Magazine advertisement for Mercier Frères, decorators and furnishers, Paris, 1929.* Shows a mock-up of an entry hall.

# 1930-1939

**The 1930s are often seen as a dismal period in twentieth-century history, with the world feeling the effects of the Great Depression, various wars, colonial expansion and the rise of authoritarian regimes. However, the decorative arts, and interiors in particular, were not diminished; they adapted to the changing circumstances arising from societal changes, the development of new materials and the changing market.**

New materials and technologies – such as tubular steel and chromium plate, sheet glass and plywood – would all contribute to an increasingly modern outlook for interior design. Many people still wanted the security of traditional imagery, but a younger generation was keen on modernity. As a consequence, in this decade we can see interiors designed in versions of Art Deco, the Moderne, Neo-Baroque, Surrealism, Eclecticism, Streamlining and the International Style, among others. In reality, however, a wide range of traditional and modern designs coexisted in most countries through the particular choices in identity and taste made by individuals.

Decorating ideas were often derived from a growing number of publications, as well as retail stores and cinema. People often translated escapist imagery of luxury interiors and lifestyles as well as extravagant sets into mediocre copies in their own homes. To meet this demand, commercial manufacturers successfully introduced versions of high-style products into the mass market for textiles, furniture, wallpaper and accessories. Designers derived forms, materials and colour imagery from an astonishing array of influences, including eighteenth-century French, ancient Egyptian, Cubist, Mayan, African and Oceanic cultures. Their products particularly reflected the fashionable imagery of the time; for example, zigzags, sunbursts and jazz patterns.

Alongside the continuing taste for a variety of eclectic and decorative interiors, the so-called International Style developed. The style, whose name was derived from the 1932 exhibition in the Museum of Modern Art in New York entitled Modern Architecture: An International Exhibition, was a challenge to traditions. Its key features, for both interiors and exteriors, included an emphasis on volumes of space, not mass; regularity rather than symmetry; use of modern materials and techniques and a rejection of applied ornament. Functionalism, industrial planning, scientific management and new materials all influenced the development of the idea that a house was "a machine for living", as termed by the architect Le Corbusier. And if the house were to be a machine, this would naturally influence its furnishing and decoration.

## BRITAIN

Interior design in Britain during this decade reflected many of these approaches. On the one hand, Wells Coates and Serge Chermayeff created interiors in the newly built offices and studios for the BBC in London in the early 1930s that embraced modern materials and simple functional lines; on the other hand, society designers such as Syrie Maugham and Cecil Beaton developed luxurious idiosyncratic interiors that emphasized style and taste for discerning clients.

Women decorators and designers were a major feature of interior design work in the 1930s. Syrie Maugham was a fashionable society decorator whose trademark was the all-white room. For example, in her own house she created an interior of stripped pine woodwork, drawing room upholstery in shades of cream and white and furniture painted off-white, all set off with a mirrored chromium screen. Well known in Britain, Maugham was also influential in the USA. Her work for Mrs Tobin Clark's bedroom in San Mateo, California, in 1930 followed the white convention that she had established, though the room had the addition of linen-covered walls patterned with a green trellis design.

Commercial interior design projects were undertaken by businesses such as those established by Betty Joel, who worked within Art Deco-inspired themes. With a showroom in Knightsbridge and a factory for furniture making, she was able to undertake interior design work for a range of corporations, hotels and showrooms as well as supplying private clients. A little later, in 1933, Lady Sibyl Colefax set up as a decorator, and from 1938 she was joined by John Fowler. This partnership was important as it responded to both a desire for authentic historic English interiors or recreations of them, as well as a more individual 'chintzy' country house look that widened the taste for that style.

The escapist mode of Art Deco design, with its shades of exoticism, luxury and glamour, was well adapted to cinemas, hotels and other commercial buildings throughout the 1930s. In England, the rooms of Eltham Palace, London, illustrate the ideal of sumptuous luxury. Built in 1936 for Stephen and Virginia Courtauld, the dining room contrasts precious woods with a silvered ceiling and fashionable pink leather upholstered dining chairs with black-and-silver doors, portraying animals and birds from London Zoo.

The effects that could be achieved through the use of mirrored glass and lighting were stunningly demonstrated by designers of the period. Oliver Hill's work for Lady Mount Temple at Gayfere House, Oliver Bernard's Strand Palace Hotel and Norris Wakefield's glass panelling and crystal chandelier work for Norman Hartnell's couture salon in London all exploited the sparkle and brilliance of these materials. Mirrors, glass in various colours and lighting effects stunningly came together in Edward James's famous commission for the bathroom in his London flat, designed for his wife Tilly Losch by Surrealist artist Paul Nash.

Ocean liners offered another interior space for the decorators' imagination to run wild. Styles ranged from Tudor country house to Italian Renaissance and from Pompeian interiors to, of course, Art Deco. The *Queen Mary* favoured an Art Deco style, criticized in the architectural press as expensive vulgarity; critics compared it unfavourably with Brian O'Rourke's work for the Orient Line's *Orion* ship, which they saw as an example of a ship fitted out in a Modern movement idiom, having no references to the past.

The London Transport system, redesigned in a Modernist manner through the efforts of Frank Pick, also provided a unified brand image. Whether it was the interior design of the headquarters of the organization, the stations or the interior fabrics of the coaches, Pick employed the best designers of the decade. The majority of Britons, however, did not regard interior design in their own homes as hugely important, so the popular taste remained rooted in an eclectic mix of traditional reproduction designs with Modern or Art Deco influences in details, accessories and wallpapers.

## GERMANY AND ITALY

In the early 1930s, the Bauhaus closed and its staff either moved away or fled Nazi Germany. Nevertheless, some interiors designed in the early 1930s demonstrated a maturing of Bauhaus ideals. For example in 1930, Marcel Breuer designed an apartment for gymnastics teacher Hilde Levi in Berlin. A clear example of function dictating form and thus creating a very particular living space, the ground floor apartment comprised a large gym space and a smaller living area with a sleeping recess, featuring a sliding dividing wall. Breuer fitted the services compactly into small auxiliary spaces.

The regime's denial of Modernism and Modern art meant that designers such as Walter Gropius, Marcel Breuer and Eric Mendelsohn left Germany and moved initially to the UK, where they had a small influence in promoting modern architecture and interior design. For example, Erich Mendelsohn and Serge Chermayeff's 1935 De La Warr Pavilion in Bexhill-on-Sea, East Sussex, is a fine example of international Modernism.

In contrast, the fascist regime in Italy adopted the ideals of Rational architecture and design as a sign of modernity and as a cleansing of the past. The famous Casa del Fascio in Como, designed by Giuseppe Terragni in 1932–36, demonstrates the stripped down and functional style, complete with interiors and specific architect-designed furniture.

**LEFT**
*De La Warr Pavilion, Bexhill-on-Sea, Sussex, designed by Erich Mendelsohn and Serge Chermayeff, 1935.* The south stairwell and lamp detail show crisp, pure Modernism.

## SCANDINAVIAN MODERNISM

In northern Europe, there was a tendency, partly derived from the philosophies of the Arts and Crafts Movement, to link human needs and their environments together. Although designers accepted Modernist ideas of improvement based on standardization of design, partly as a better way to meet society's needs, changes in social attitudes were also fundamental to the provision of a better everyday life for people. The 1923 Gothenburg Exhibition revealed that Sweden was able to merge design and artisanship successfully to create attractive and liveable interiors.

In 1930, the Stockholm Exhibition again showed the world what Swedish design in particular meant – a restrained Modernism informed by a craft ethic which placed emphasis on the user's needs and desires. Based on humanitarian and social practices, this approach was different to pure and unfamiliar expressions of particular theoretical considerations. It seemed to recognize the importance of designing with people in mind, hence the emphasis on appropriate size, cost and quality. This approach particularly applied to interior design.

An example of the above can be seen in Svenskt Tenn, Stockholm's interior design store established in the 1920s. The business developed in the 1930s through the

**BELOW**

*Country living room shown in the Swedish Pavilion, International Exhibition, Paris, 1937.*

*The setting showed the Swedish approach to design with a human touch and an emphasis on comfort over style.*

collaboration between owner Estrid Ericson and Austrian émigré Josef Frank. Frank's vision of human Modernism in his designs for furniture and patterned textiles were a recipe for success. Svenskt Tenn went on to exhibit in the Paris exhibition of 1937 and in New York in 1939, demonstrating the Swedish modern furnishing idiom.

Probably the best-known Scandinavian architect and designer of the period was the Finn Alvar Aalto. Although known for many architectural and decorative arts projects, his Vipuri Library (1935) and Villa Mairea (1937–39) epitomized his approach to humanistic design. The design of Villa Mairea incorporates a number of elements that link tradition with modernity. Timber poles from the ceiling to the floor act as boundaries, as in traditional farmhouses, but also reflect the forest outside. Aalto also contrasts sharply delineated forms with relaxing wave-like shapes that appear in harmony. Indeed his interest in the free-form curved line as a representation of humanity as opposed to the mechanical is seen throughout much of his work for interiors and products.

## USA

Although the United States had suffered in the great financial crash of 1929 and the subsequent depression, the period was also a catalyst for a new wave of building and development. A revitalized design scene that demonstrated the eclectic nature of American taste in interiors was seen in 1932–33: the New York Museum of Modern Art opened the exhibition The International Style, which showcased Modernism; the restored eighteenth-century Colonial Williamsburg site opened and the 1933 Century of Progress exhibition in Chicago became a setting for the display of Art Deco and Streamlining.

The immigration of European Modernists such as Mies van der Rohe, Marcel Breuer

**LEFT**
*Radio City Music Hall private apartment for the manager by Donald Deskey, 1933.* This apartment is furnished with cherry wood panelling, and furniture featuring brushed aluminium and Bakelite.

**ABOVE LEFT**

*A room in the Guest House, Fallingwater, Bear Run, Penn, by Frank Lloyd Wright, 1935–37 (Guest House 1939). The integration of the site with the interiors is evident in the choice of materials.*

**ABOVE RIGHT**

*Entrance to apartment, Hampshire House, New York West side, by Dorothy Draper, 1937. The bold plasterwork, large scale doors and chequered floor reflect elements of the English country house look.*

and Walter Gropius gave impetus to the development of Modernism in architecture and interior design in the USA. The Philadelphia Savings Fund Society building (1931–32) was the first truly International Style skyscraper in the USA. Designed by George Howe and Swiss immigrant William Lescaze, it was unashamedly modern and luxurious. The banking hall had interiors of grey, white and black marble, including the floors. The columns and counters were relieved by blue upholstered chromium chairs and tubular steel frames to the desks, designed by the architects.

The attraction of Art Deco and its associated links with streamlining – the use of curved shapes and aerodynamic imagery that reflected a relaxed modernity – were demonstrated early in the decade. The concentration on styling and design without too many moral overtones, an espousal of the aesthetic of speed and colour and inspiration from Futurist and Expressionist art movements were the hallmarks of this approach. Pioneering industrial designers including Walter Dorwin Teague, Donald Deskey, Norman Bel Geddes, Henry Dreyfuss and Raymond Loewy were instrumental in promoting the style in both products and interiors, particularly for transport. Ships, trains and planes were all subject to makeovers in this period and, of course, this influenced public taste. In particular, Henry Dreyfuss's *20th Century Limited* train gave travellers a taste of the new style. The train's ribbed, coloured and polished metals, venetian blinds and blue leather upholstery (all within a grey colour scheme), along with the use of new materials such as plastic laminates and Flexwood, fully expressed modernity. Donald Deskey's contribution to the Radio City Music Hall in New York (1932–33) was another important example of streamlined modernity. He encapsulated the style through his use of mirrors, furniture of aluminium and chrome-plated steel furniture, in conjunction with plastic laminates, lacquer finishes and patterned wallpapers in colourful schemes.

In other areas of decoration and interior design, particularly the domestic, there was a growing appreciation of antiques and interiors based on accurate historic interpretations. Antiques were often combined with other styles and an eclectic 'good taste' developed in certain quarters, promoted particularly by women decorators from the previous decades, including Elsie De Wolfe, Ruby Ross Wood, Rose Cumming and Nancy McClelland. In this decade, too, additional businesses entered the fray and interior decorators, such as McMillen Inc., Dorothy Draper, Mrs Henry Parish II and Frances Elkins, were creating highly fashionable interiors.

At the same time, American males working in the decorating field included important designers such as Edward Wormley and T. H. Robsjohn-Gibbings, who were especially influential in furniture design; William Pahlmann, whose eclectic and theatrical style was often showcased in model interiors for the Lord and Taylor store in New York, that contrasted with the historicism of many other decorators of that time and Billy Baldwin, who initially worked for Ruby Ross Wood and was eventually to become a major master of interior decoration in his own right.

**BELOW**
*Work area in the Johnson Wax Building, headquarters of the S. C. Johnson and Son, Racine, Wisconsin, by Frank Lloyd Wright, 1936–39.*

Another fascinating development in the United States was the resurgence of Frank Lloyd Wright. Always an individualist, two of his greatest buildings were created in this decade. The inspirational Fallingwater at Bear Run near Pittsburgh, commissioned by Edgar Kaufmann as a weekend home, was completed in 1936. The combination of concrete-cantilevered planes over the waterfall, with an organic interior embedded into the rugged site was unique. The contrasts, which it offers within a complete building, show Wright's management of nature, craft, industrial techniques and a superb sense of place. In a different idiom, Wright developed the open-plan office concept with his project for the S. C. Johnson & Son administration building in Racine, Wisconsin (1936–39). It was a stunning success with a combination of brick, glass and metal components that expressed a streamlined modernity, though in an inimitable style. Again, Wright controlled every detail of the project, including the well-known furniture of wood and rust-coloured metal intended to blend with the exposed brickwork.

## FRANCE

In France, the twin tracks of Modernism and a later Art Deco style are also evident. Pierre Chareau's Maison de Verre (1932) was a building and interior that represented Modernism through its use of industrial-type materials, including glass blocks for walls, exposed steel frameworks painted red, black metal shelving for bookcases and hard rubber flooring. Oddly, it had traditional upholstered settees covered in tapestries designed by the painter Jean Lurçat. Clearly, the effect was intended to be stylish but not to create a 'manifesto space', i.e., an interior that was a statement of a position rather than a true living space.

Meanwhile, Jean-Michel Frank developed a very particular style of interior design that led him to be one of France's most celebrated interior designers – the salon in Vicomte Charles de Noailles home in Paris exemplifies this. Always interested in creating a total interior, he worked closely with Adolphe Chanaux as well as numerous artists and makers who supplied his business with the luxurious furnishings that he required. Although loosely linked to Art Deco style, Frank identified with simplicity and costly sophistication, most notably in his choice of materials and textures. An idea of his influential role in interiors of the 1930s is found in his connections with designers including Eleanor Brown, Syrie Maugham, Frances Elkins and Elsie de Wolfe.

In this decade traditional and modern decoration sat equally, though uneasily, beside each other: it was fashionably acceptable to have a taste that reflected either of these extremes or any of the many variations that could be created inbetween.

**ABOVE**
*The Maison de Verre, Paris,*
*by Pierre Chareau, 1928–32.*
*The double-height interior*
*demonstrates the use of*
*industrial materials includ-*
*ing glass bricks and exposed*
*steel girders.*

**RIGHT**
*Design for a living and writing room by Professor Paul Griesser, Bielefeld, 1930.*

**BELOW**
*Illustration of the exercise room at Elizabeth Arden's showroom Fifth Avenue, New York, from Fortune magazine, 1930.*

**OPPOSITE**
*Lobby of the Empire State Building, New York, 1931 (renovated 2009). The 'lost' ceiling mural depicted a sky with sunbursts and stars that resembled industrial gears and wheels.*

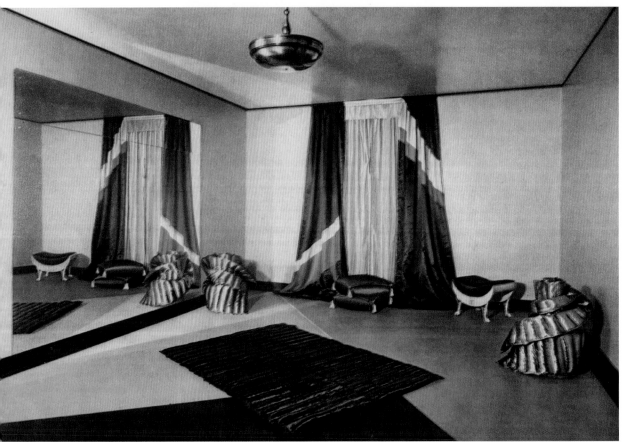

**RIGHT**
*Bedroom in the Bergmann Haus,
Dresden, by Bruno Paul, 1930.*

**RIGHT**
*Dressing room with mural deco-
ration in house of artist Fritz Paul
Blum, by Bruno Paul, 1930.*

*Living space in the Villa Savoye, Poissy, nr. Paris, 1929-31, by Le Corbusier.* This master-piece of modernist design demonstrates not only his 'five points' of architecture but also the plan of the house around the central courtyard allowing both an open plan and circulation through the spaces

**BELOW**
*Office designed by the company DIM (Décoration Intérieure Moderne) with macassar ebony cabinets and parchment walls, 1930.*

**OPPOSITE ABOVE**
Dining room by Georges Djo-
Bourgeois with textiles by Elise
Djo-Bourgeois, 1930.

**OPPOSITE BELOW LEFT**
Living area by Maurice Dufrène,
1930. Table and Chairs feature black patent leather.

**OPPOSITE BELOW RIGHT**
Dining room by Maurice Jallot
with furniture in Persian walnut
and sharkskin, 1930.

**ABOVE LEFT**
Advertisement for Edgar Brandt's
artistic ironwork business, Paris,
in L'Illustration magazine, 1931.

**LEFT**
Boudoir by Louis Sognot with
typical Art Deco features including a small leopard sculpture,
1930.

**ABOVE**
*The lobby to the Daily Express
building in Fleet Street, London,
designed by Robert Atkinson,
1932.* A flamboyant and
highly crafted Art Deco
interior.

**ABOVE**

*The theatre in Radio City complex in New York, designed by Donald Deskey in 1932.* The building has a series of overlapping shell shapes that form the celling, all illuminated with cove lights. Furniture and fittings incorporate glass, aluminum, chrome and leather.

**ABOVE**
*Room designed for the General Electric Company showing various kinds of lighting, 1933.*

**LEFT**
*Living room designed by John Duncan Miller for Curtis Moffat, 1933.* This room demonstrates the decorative quality of sycamore veneer.

**LEFT**
*A Bedroom in the Maison de Verre, Paris, by Pierre Chareau, 1928-32.* The wall with a solid base, clear centre and opaque top windows shows Chareau's attention to detail in arranging a room.

TWENTIETH CENTURY INTERIORS ••• 1930-1939

**ABOVE**
*Living room designed by Betty Joel, 1933.* Illustrates how successfully a monochrome scheme can be created.

**RIGHT**
*Living room designed by John Duncan Miller, 1933.* A simple beige scheme is enlivened by accents of colour.

**OPPOSITE**
*A music room, designed by artists Duncan Grant and Vanessa Bell, 1933.*

**RIGHT**
*Axel Larsson plywood magazine cabinet and chair, Sweden, 1933.*

**BELOW**
*Living room designed by Ronald Dickens, 1933.* The boxed-in fireplace modernized the old-fashioned fireplace.

**LEFT**
*Living room designed by*
*Betty Joel, 1933.* The walls are
panelled in Canadian pine
and much of the furniture is
in sycamore.

**LEFT**
*A suggestion for a workroom*
*or study designed by Rodney*
*Thomas for Mr Ashley Havinden,*
*1933.*

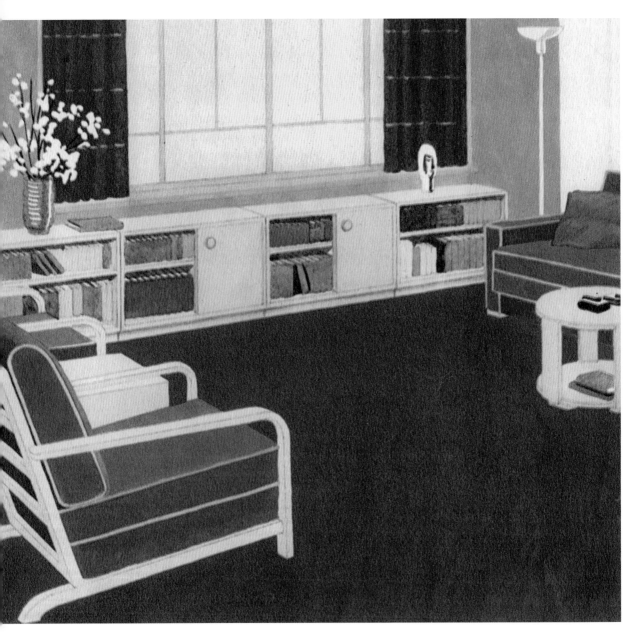

**ABOVE**
*Gilbert Rohde, Three Way Room,
from Fortune magazine, 1935.*

**LEFT**

*Mock-up of design office by Raymond Loewy displayed in design exhibition at the Metropolitan Museum in New York, 1934.* The elegant streamlined interior complete with tubular steel furniture radiated the idea of modernity.

**BELOW**

*Jean Rothschild upholstered chairs with needlepoint tapestry by Gaudissart for the Grand Salon of the liner Normandie, 1934.*

**ABOVE**
*Dressing room created by Cedric Gibbons, William Horning and E.B. Willis, for the MGM Hollywood movie Wife vs. Secretary, 1936.*

**LEFT**

*Dining room created by Cedric
Gibbons, William Horning and
E.B. Willis, for the MGM Hollywood movie Wife vs. Secretary,
1936.*

**LEFT**

*Cocktail bar created by Cedric
Gibbons, William Horning and
E.B. Willis, for the MGM Hollywood movie Wife vs. Secretary,
1936.*

**RIGHT**

*The living room of the newly refurbished Future House at Rockefeller Center, New York, 1936.* This room shows unit furniture that can be purchased one piece at a time.

**BELOW**

*A games room with sectional furniture seating units and naïve murals, 1936.*

**BELOW**
*Simple kitchen with refrigerator
taking pride of place, 1936.*

**OPPOSITE**

*Interior Court of the Johnson Wax Company Building, Racine (Wisconsin), by Frank Lloyd Wright, 1936-9.* The squat mushroom shaped columns and capitals reflect the larger versions in the main office space.

**LEFT**

*The Assembly Hall of the Casa Del Fascio, Como, Italy, by Giuseppe Terragni, 1932-6.* The rationalist design has a double height atrium and a glass roof over the large open space intended for public events. When the space was inadequate, for the numbers, the gates could be removed completely merging the interior and exterior spaces, plaza and atrium

**OPPOSITE**
*Ensemble by Eugène Printz, 1937.*
*Art Deco-style vertical*
*emphasis.*

**FAR LEFT**
*The study and hallway in Walter*
*Gropius's house, Lincoln, Mass.,*
*1937–38. Bauhaus Modern-*
*ism on a domestic scale.*

**LEFT**
*Gropius's house, Lincoln,*
*Mass., 1937–38. The curved*
*staircase , a favoured New*
*England device, suggests a*
*private upper level.*

**BELOW**
*Treatment for an oval-shaped*
*bedroom by André Arbus, 1937.*

**RIGHT**

*Kitchen designed for a small house by Mrs Darcy Braddell at the Paris International Exhibition, 1937.*

**RIGHT**

*Office designed by Louis Sognot, 1937.*

**LEFT**
*Living room designed by Ross Stewart for W & J Sloane of New York, 1938.*

**BELOW**
*Showroom display of a living room by Ross Stewart for W & J Sloane, New York, 1938.*

**RIGHT**

*A suggestion for an inexpensive dining room by Betty Joel Ltd, London, 1938.*

**RIGHT**

*A modern dining room for the country by Serge Chermayeff and Erich Mendelsohn, Dell & Wainwright, London, 1938.*

**LEFT**
*Serge Chermayeff dining room
with MR10 chairs by Mies van der
Rohe, 1938.*

**ABOVE**
*Modern treatment for attic living room designed by Hartigan Ltd., London, 1938.*

**ABOVE LEFT**
*Living space designed by John Gerald for the B. Altman department store, New York, 1938.*

**ABOVE RIGHT**
*Room designed by Russel Wright, 1938.* Green and white wallpaper, maple furniture, a heavily textured rug in grey and green wool, white chenille and chromium lamps.

**RIGHT**
*Suggestion for bachelor girl's bedroom by Derek Patmore for Drages Ltd., London, 1938.*

**ABOVE**

*A covered terrace by Hayes Marshall for Fortnum & Mason Ltd., London, with Finnish birch furniture, 1938.*

**LEFT**

*Simple living room designed by Axel Larsson, 1939. The room is furnished with Swedish Modern furniture and furnishings. The illustration is from a publication celebrating ten years of Swedish craft and handicrafts.*

**ABOVE**
*The entrance hall at 2 Willow Road, designed by Ernö Goldfinger, 1939.* This shows the opaque glass wall with compartments displaying vases and various objects.

**ABOVE**

*Sitting room and balcony at 2*
*Willow Road, Hampstead, Lon-*
*don, by Ernö Goldfinger, 1939.*
The contrast with the view
of the terraced houses in the
background is startling.

# 1940-1949

World War II and its aftermath dominated the 1940s, having a serious impact on design. The War and other major upheavals of the time were also to have effects in the longer term. For example, the results of scientific and technological advances that took place during the period influenced developments in interiors, both materially and stylistically. The development of plastics and synthetic fibres was one direct influence on the sector, but other advances as diverse as the study of atomic molecular structure and the development of television, synthetic rubber and computers brought about changes in both commercial and domestic interiors.

During this decade, interior design continued to be a business that catered for a wide variety of styles and tastes. Modernism developed in two ways: the geometric and the organic. The keywords "efficiency" and "technology" clearly linked Modernist concepts to contemporary society. The geometric style, based on Bauhaus teaching, came to the fore in the USA, where many of the Bauhaus faculty had established themselves. The style seemed to represent a new start in the USA-led West, especially in terms of commercial development, i.e. the office block and the factory. Geometric Modernism was a flagship for the brave new world of technologies, standardization and production, along with the application of new materials. Indeed, in a reversal of the previous decades, America became world leader in innovations in interiors, while Europe, with some exceptions, trailed. Scandinavia continued to exert a benign influence on interiors and furniture, while at the end of the decade Italian designers began to have an impact.

The other development of Modernism was in the direction of the organic rather than the mechanic, something that continued into the 1950s. The influence of fine art, especially the work of Picasso, Miró, Arp and Calder, directed designers towards an organic modernism that employed amoeba-like shapes, for example, as the basis for tables, chairs and textile patterns. This approach was somewhat at odds with the machine aesthetic of the International Style, but a number of countries espoused it. In Italy, for example, it was a reaction to the association of the Modern movement with Fascism, while in Britain it reflected the interest in science studies along with a continuing mainstream rejection of angular Modernism. Whether in Jackson Pollock's or Joan Miró's art works, Czechoslovakian glassware, British textiles or American furniture, the influence of the organic was clear.

## USA

As suggested above, the USA had taken the lead in the world of modern art and design, so it's perhaps unsurprising that many American designers were at the forefront of innovative developments. One particularly interesting initiative

was the Case Study House programme, which ran from 1945 to the mid-1960s. It was sponsored by John Entenza and his *Arts & Architecture* magazine. Entenza commissioned important architects and designers, including Richard Neutra, Charles and Ray Eames, Pierre Koenig and Eero Saarinen, to develop their ideas with a view to influencing the boom in house-building following World War II. The buildings created were therefore trials of low-cost and efficient housing. Most of the projects were completed in the Los Angeles area and one of the most well known was Case Study House No. 8, also known as the Eames House.

The Eames House, circa 1945–49, home to Charles and Ray Eames, was built in California with a steel frame on a modular grid, using easily available industrial components. It had exposed metal finishes in contrast to wood cladding, with plywood panels and painted plaster. Although an interesting precursor of the hi-tech style of the 1970s, it was most remarkable as a receptacle of the Eames's own collection of accessories

**ABOVE**
*Farnsworth House, Plano, Illinois by Mies van der Rohe, 1945–51.* *This iconic single level house offers a Platonic view of the concept of the 'dwelling' through the minimal structure and deployment of space.*

that reflected the life and lifestyle of the occupants. The juxtaposition of Eames's furniture with oriental objects, toys and ethnic crafts, along with found objects and artworks, demonstrates how an interior environment works to reflect the identity of the owners.

The near contemporaneous building of Philip Johnson's Glass House of 1949, which reflected a Miesian ideal, and Mies van der Rohe's own project, his Farnsworth House of 1951, reveal the epitome of high Modernism in architectural design. The use of modern materials including steel and glass, the concept of 'less is more', and the connection between a building and its site are all explicit in these houses. In the Glass House, Johnson used Barcelona and Brno chairs designed by Mies van der Rohe in the 1920s, upholstered in natural pigskin, a Mies flat couch and bolster in black, along with a white wool area rug, itself sitting on a polished, dark brick floor. With limited but exclusive accessories, the room was a showcase for Modernist ideals. Interestingly, Farnsworth House, designed by Mies, was furnished with Scandinavian products and was, therefore, less of a total work of art than that of Johnson, Mies's protégé.

These houses were never intended to be family homes, and their stark modernity gave rise to some criticism in some circles. The editor of *House Beautiful* magazine (April

**BELOW**
*Terrace Plaza Hotel restaurant, Cincinnati, by Skidmore, Owings & Merrill, 1948.* The architects designed the restaurant's interiors and accessories, and commissioned Joan Miró to design a mural as a focal point for the gourmet restaurant.

**LEFT**
*Terrace Plaza Hotel restaurant, Cincinnati, 1948, by Skidmore, Owings & Merrill.* A view of the restaurant appearing colourful but strangely lifeless without the diners.

**BELOW**
*A display from the Organic Design in Home Furnishings competition held at the Museum of Modern Art, New York, 1940–41.* The entries by Eero Saarinen and Charles Eames both won first prize in the storage and seating categories.

1953) used Farnsworth House as an example of un-American design that was seen as a threat to individuality. She suggested that International Stylists, who were themselves émigrés, were forcing this type of inhuman, impractical and ugly design upon Americans. In any event, both these examples are exceptional, though many of the ideas used were taken and diluted for other works.

Influential on the commercial scene, Skidmore Owings & Merrill (SOM) was a large architectural firm who had established an important interior design department in the mid-1940s, a trend not surprising given the Modernist emphasis on the concept of a total work of art. In this case, the architects were re-embracing their role as designers of spaces as well as of buildings. One interior they designed was the Terrace Plaza Hotel in Cincinnati, a project led by architect and designer Natalie de Blois and fitted out with custom furniture designed by the firm's Benjamin Baldwin and Ward Bennett, murals painted by Miró and Steinberg and a mobile by Alexander Calder; even the small details such as china and uniforms were considered part of the designer's remit.

Another significant trend during the 1940s was the interest in organic Modernism. Although already developed through the work of Alvar Aalto and Frank Lloyd Wright

**RIGHT**
*Fefe's Monte Carlo club in New York designed by Dorothy Draper, c.1942.* This nightclub has lush drapery in chartreuse satin and cardinal-red velvet fitted behind the scrolled blackberry-coloured banquette.

**OPPOSITE**
*Woodland Crematorium , Stockholm, Gunnar Asplund, 1940.* This view shows part of the interior with plywood panels on the wall that appear to peal away to create seating. A challenging technical process that appears completely natural.

during the 1930s, it was in this decade that it was accepted as a mainstream style. In 1940, the Museum of Modern Art in New York sponsored and hosted the Organic Design in Home Furnishing competition and exhibition, which attracted a number of important designers including Charles Eames and Eero Saarinen. They collaborated on the design of shaped plywood chairs and modular storage elements that both won awards. By the middle of the decade, Charles and Ray Eames's work on moulded plywood chairs had created a new interpretation of the chair. In a period of great inventiveness, they had not only developed the shaped plywood chair but also others featuring fibreglass and steel frames and the avant-garde "Aluminium Group" of seating.

Although "organic" in this context usually refers to the shape of components, it can also refer to the material of the interior. Alexander Girard, a designer of domestic and commercial interiors in this period, exemplified the wartime use of simple organic materials and textures to create interesting interiors. In his own office showroom in Detroit, built in 1946–47, he used natural plywood for the walls, natural jute for the wall covering and black painted fibreboard panels for the ceiling, all set off by tan-coloured carpeting.

While these initiatives took place, the decorators maintained a position as arbiters of fashionable taste. The interior decorator Dorothy Draper had a syndicated newspaper column, wrote for *Good Housekeeping*, published books and had her own radio show called *Lines about Living*. In 1941 she was appointed director of the *Good Housekeeping* Studio of Architectural Building and Furnishing. Apart from these publishing ventures, she continued to create important interiors, including the Mayflower Hotel, Washington (1940) and the Modern Baroque Coty salon on Fifth Avenue, New York (1943).

Designer and decorator Tony Duquette represents an interesting crossover in interior work and film set design. Initially planning in-store displays, in 1940 he was commissioned by Elsie de Wolfe to propose furniture for her Beverley Hills home. Soon after that, he was called on to design film sets for important movies such as *Ziegfeld Follies* (1946) and Fred Astaire's *Yolanda and the Thief* (1945). Later his work carried him to a wide range of locations and famous clients, while he also designed a range of jewellery and textiles sold under his label – one way that decorators developed their sphere of influence and remained well known within particular circles.

The Scandinavian influence continued in the USA and elsewhere, especially in the export of furniture and textiles for home furnishings. One particular interior from Stockholm, Sweden, is noteworthy: Gunnar Asplund's Woodland Crematorium of 1940. Although the whole site of the crematorium is a UNESCO World Heritage Site, the interior design alone is praiseworthy. As a link between Swedish vernacular and restrained Modernism, it is a classic example. The nature of the building has been considered in terms of the removal of distractions from the mourning process, so the furniture of the chapels (three in total) was designed to be simple but comfortable, with high-quality materials and finishes.

The Scandinavian influence was probably at work in the interiors of the Bay Region in California at this time. The style, which was a particular American West Coast rejection of international Modernism, was more humane in scale and use of materials and respected the vernacular traditions. A classic example that demonstrates this approach is the Weston Havens House, designed in 1940 by architect Harwell Hamilton Harris for the philanthropist John Weston Havens Jr. The surfaces and materials used for the interior include unfinished redwood, natural rush matting, floor to ceiling windows and walls of books. Furniture by Scandinavian designers including Alvar Aalto and Bruno Mathsson made the link with organic humanist design as opposed to International Style modernism.

## BRITAIN

For Britain, the decade was mainly remembered as one of rationing, 'make do and mend', and the government-controlled Utility scheme for furniture and furnishings. Although there was an ember of whimsy and frivolity in the second half of the decade, it was rare. The Utility scheme had some merit in that it controlled production of furnishings and made them available to those in most need, and it also encouraged the design of simpler furniture and furnishings. The products were influenced by the Arts and Crafts Movement's ideals, in conjunction with a restrained Modernism that was seen, in a younger generation, as important in breaking the hold of tradition on British

**BELOW**
*Display of Prototype Utility furniture, Britain, c.1946.*
*The Utility scheme was initially introduced to manage scarce resources, but it was later used to try and influence design taste in the British public. This example shows a restrained Modernism with Arts and Crafts influences.*

design. Because of this approach, variations on the image of simple furniture, white walls and gingham curtains was evident in many room sets, illustrations and photo shoots.

In 1946, the newly established Council of Industrial Design sponsored the *Britain Can Make It* exhibition, held in London, which showed a range of products, including a number of furnished room settings. These were of great interest, but as they were not widely available, the public remained frustrated. The establishment of the Council's publication *Design* in 1949 continued to spread the gospel of "good design". At a grass roots level, and arguably more realistically, the book *Modern Homes Illustrated*, published in 1947, suggested that homemakers should choose from a range of furnishing opportunities including built-in, antique, reproduction, Utility, garden and painted furniture. Clearly this was a response to the state of the country following the war. Nevertheless, the book showed consumers a whole range of ideas and illustrations of new products and home design solutions even if some of them were not available at the time. However, it was not until 1951, with the Festival of Britain, that a new spirit really entered British interior design.

## ITALY

After the war, there was a marked change in Italian design. The period after 1945, often called the *ricostruzione*, led to a variety of styles, including an approach influenced by Modernist developments in America and specific Italian style called Neo-Liberty,

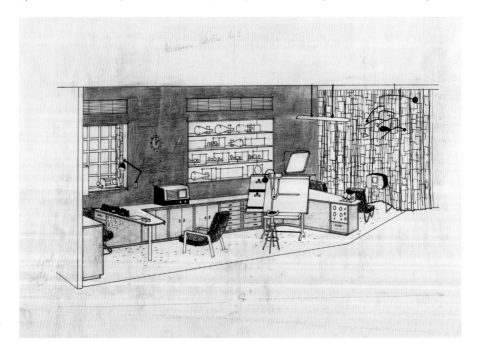

**RIGHT**
*Design for a television research engineer's office by Christopher Nicholson, 1946. This office was designed for the Britain Can Make It exhibition, held at the Victoria & Albert Museum, South Kensington, London.*

which referred to a design position that borrowed elements of Art Nouveau and which enabled designers to link with a more organic imagery. One of the most interesting designers to engage with the latter, organic, approach was Carlo Mollino. He worked on aeroplanes and racing car projects as well as architecture, interiors and furniture. Among a number of apartments he designed, Mollino's work from 1949 for the Marquis Vladi Orengo's apartment, the Casa Orengo in Turin, was particularly interesting. It incorporated Surrealistic spaces with specially produced furniture and furnishings that displayed Mollino's attraction to eroticism and the human form.

**BELOW**
*Occasional table for the Casa Orengo, designed by Carlo Mollino, 1949.* Made from maple-faced plywood, glass, and brass by Apelli e Varesio, Turin, the table demonstrates Mollino's organic style.

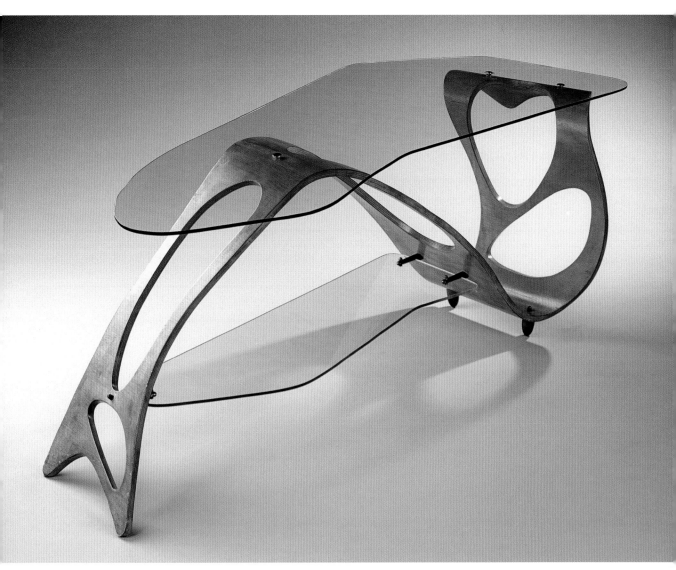

## FRANCE

In France, although *haute couture* appeared to take pride of place in the design hierarchy, there was a revival of the opulent grand schemes of the past in some of the wealthy artistic houses. Charles de Beistegui's Parisian townhouse was the epitome of this taste with its over-scaled and opulent furniture and fittings in a Baroque taste. Although architects such as Jean Prouvé began to develop new ideas in French furnishings, most clients were still drawn to tradition. After the war, the 1930s decorator Jean Royère founded his own company and decided to expand the business into the lucrative Middle Eastern market, with branches in Lebanon, Egypt and Syria. He had a unique style that was bold in the use of colour, materials and textures, though it was somewhat outside of the mainstream. His work included palaces for clients such as  King Farouk, King Hussein of Jordan, and the Shah of Iran.

## AUSTRALIA

Between 1946 and 1948, the Austrian émigré Harry Seidler was chief assistant to Marcel Breuer in his New York office. In 1948, he left for Australia, where he built the famous Rose Seidler House for his parents. Introducing Bauhaus-inspired Modernist architecture to Australia, the house demonstrates the Modernist axioms of open plan, elegant simplicity of finishes and layout, as well as accepting that technology was an important part of a modern lifestyle. The house integrated many instances of labour-saving devices, built-in equipment and storage facilities as well as contemporary furniture from designers such as Eames and Saarinen.

The year 1950 can be considered the end of an era in more ways than one. It was this year that saw the deaths of three doyennes of the interior design world: Ruby Ross Wood, Elsie de Wolfe and Sibyl Colefax. More significantly, it marked the beginning of both the consolidation of Modernism and the beginnings of the influence of mass culture that was to open the doors to pluralism in the coming decades.

**LEFT**

*An anteroom by Jean Royère, 1949.* The squared raffia wall panels with bamboo beading are typical of this designer's slightly unconventional approach to interiors.

**OPPOSITE**

*A room in Weston Havens House in Berkeley, California, by Harwell Hamilton Harris, 1940–41.* The room demonstrates the influence of the Japanese structures in southern California, through the designer's use of wood and his fostering of visible structural details.

**LEFT**

*Fireplace in a French country house by Jean Royère, 1940s.* The unusual wall finish of thatched straw adds a rustic note here, alongside the fireplace of old tiles.

**BELOW**

*Living room in France, 1940s.* The Art Deco–influenced furniture sets off the large tapestry.

**ABOVE**
*LLiving room in Patricia Detring's home, Bel-Air, California, 1940s.* The green chenille upholstery fits around the window with two black lacquer end tables.

**ABOVE**
*Exhibition living room by Esmé
Gordon, 1940s.* An eclectic mix
of contemporary furniture
and a reproduction Persian
carpet are shown in this
mock-up of a room.

**ABOVE**
*The Oval Room at the Hotel Pierre, New York, by Samuel Marx, 1942.* This night spot has oyster white walls and slate grey carpeting, which is offset by large, wide-perspective murals.

**RIGHT**
*The Patio restaurant, Hotel Netherland Plaza, Cincinnati, by Jac Lessman, c.1942.* The room has rattan furniture, and a lava stone floor, creating a tropical image. The lighting changed during the day, with sunlight effects for lunch, sunset for dinner and moonlight for supper.

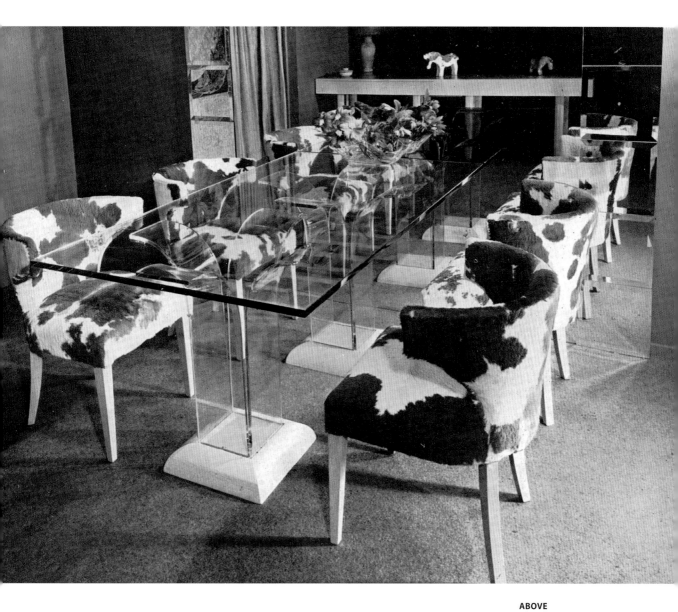

**RIGHT**
*Platform at the Stalin factory station on the Moscow Metro ((now Avtozavodskaya station) by Alexey Dushkin, 1943.* The columns and walls are clad in pinkish mottled Oraktuoy marble.

**ABOVE**
*A bedroom in a medley of shades
of yellow, 1945.* The furniture
shown here, designed by
Michel Dufet, is covered
in grey horse leather; the
wallpaper is by Dumas.

**RIGHT**
*A maquette for a sleeping and eating space by Djo Bourgeois, 1945.* An example of stripped but rigorous Modernism.

**RIGHT**
*Dining area by René Drouin, 1945.* This is an interesting dining room with aluminium alloy fittings that have been tinted yellow-gold through a process of oxidation.

**OPPOSITE**
*An office space by Michel Dufet, 1945.* This office was designed specially 'for an eminent personality of international journalism'. Note the world map, library and globe-shaped light.

**RIGHT**

*Dining room in a flat in Knightsbridge, London, c.1946.* The mural by Beatrice Mac-Dermott, depicts a Venetian scene framed in a wall panel. The room demonstrates the continuing use of mural decoration along with individual and eclectic furnishings.

**OPPOSITE**

*Cocktail bar designed by Tessiere, 1940s.* This corner of a room with faux sunblind and painted iron furniture suggests a café environment.

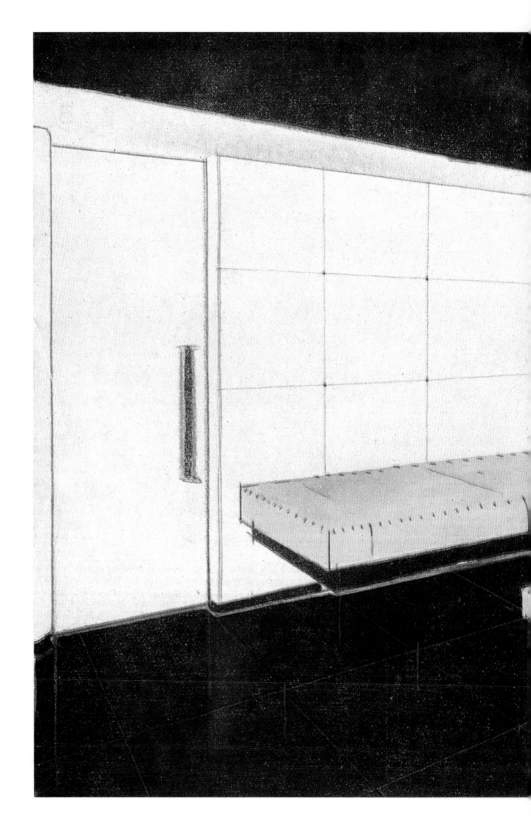

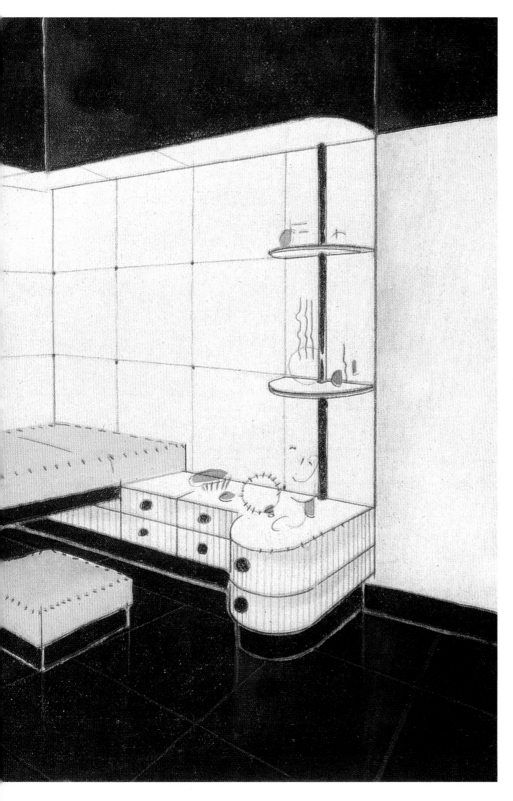

**LEFT**
*A maquette for a bathroom by d'Eaubonne, 'décorateur de cinéma', 1945.* This shows the area of the bathroom re-served for fitness, complete with black floor and white ceramic tiled walls.

**LEFT**
*The living room in Casa M-1 by Carlo Mollino, Turin, 1946.* The enlarged lithographic illustration on the wall create a backdrop to the iconic biomorphic upholstered chairs.

**RIGHT**
*A living room display by R. D. Russell, 1946.* Shown in the Furnished Room Section, of the Britain Can Make It exhibition, held at the Victoria and Albert Museum, South Kensington, London.

**ABOVE**

*An American study bedroom, 1947.* A comfortable adaptation of Modernism for a single person.

**RIGHT**

*Bar in a New York penthouse by William Pahlmann, 1948.* Home bars were fashionable in this period. This one is made from mahogany with cast bronze legs, and back-to-bar taxi-cab seats.

**OPPOSITE**

*Bedroom furnished by Bird Iles Ltd, 1948.* A 'decorator' scheme in cream, brown and ice- blue, with furniture in maple and lace mahogany.

**OVERLEAF**

*The Rose Seidler House, Wahroonga, Australia, 1948–50.* Designed by Harry Seidler for his mother, the house features Modernist ideas including open-plan living spaces and built-in fitments. The mural on the sun deck relieves a plain, muted colour scheme.

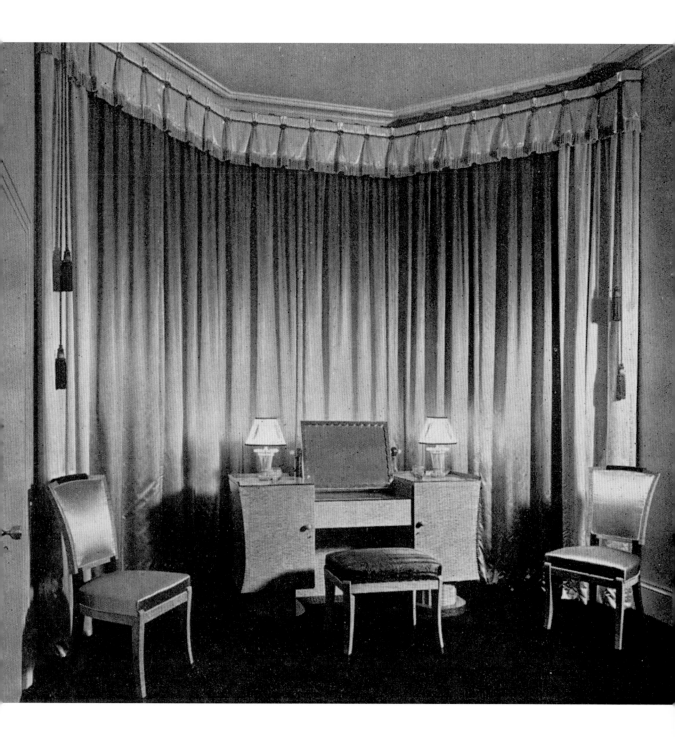

**ABOVE**

*Living room in house in Thorn-
crest Village, Ontario, by E.S.C.
Cox, 1940s.* Local stone combined with birch plywood
panels set off the standard
Canadian furniture.

**ABOVE**
*Living room in Tierra Caliente, Palm Springs, by Raymond Loewy, c.1949.*
The master bedroom in designer Loewy's own home decorated in a chocolate and corn-yellow scheme with grey carpet fitted to the pool's edge.

LEFT

**Bedroom in a house in Amsterdam by Asscher, 1940s.** *The birchwood furniture is offset by a pink and ivory colour scheme. The debt to the Art Deco style is evident in the forms of the furniture and the finishes.*

**ABOVE**

*Furnishing scheme with contemporary furniture, by Morris and Co., Glasgow, 1949.* The use of plywood and laminated processes for creating decorative effects was a speciality of this firm.

**OPPOSITE**

*Living room in an apartment by William Pahlmann, c.1940s.* The colour scheme is based on a collection of pre-Inca pottery, whilst the handwoven blinds are by Dorothy Liebes and the radiogram is covered in Di-Noc laminate material.

**ABOVE**
*A New York apartment by Eliza-
beth Draper, c.1949. A space
for entertaining, this space
had a crimson and pink
colour scheme, furnished
with selected antiques and
modern upholstery.*

**LEFT**
*A New York apartment by Elizabeth Draper, c.1949.* This space offered a formal background for small gatherings. The tole chandelier makes a dramatic statement while the hidden lights behind the unlined fabric create a soft light effect.

**RIGHT**

*Dining room by Carlo Mollino, 1949.* The window-like mural, mirrored alcove and fluorescent light, along with Mollino's very particular furniture designs, create an idiosyncratic interior.

**BELOW**

*Breakfast room suite by W & J Sloane, 1949.* The suite is of wrought iron decorated in white, chartreuse and powder pink.

*A New York perfume salon by James Amster, c.1949.* The colour scheme for the D'Orsay perfume showroom was based on crimson and French blue with black walls and white shutters and railings with Louis XV furniture.

**LEFT**
*Offices of interior designers Claiborne, Read and Pate, Dallas, c.1949.* Mr Pate's office has Regency and Empire furniture set against a background of classic draperies, with the walls panelled in antique mirror squares.

# 1950-1959

This decade was generally a period of confidence, where new notions in art, design and architecture fed the expanding world of consumerism. The so-called Contemporary style was a breath of fresh air, which in the case of some architectural developments was expressed in the buildings through features such as picture windows and open-plan layouts. There was a tendency towards, lighter and slighter furniture and lighting styles, which contrasted with the older heavy tastes that were prevalent in many pre-war homes and offices. Scandinavia and Italy were leading this style revolution, although many other countries were developing their own interpretations, too. Importantly, these ideas linked, in some cases, to Modernist thinking about function and technology so that elements such as built-in wardrobes or fitted kitchens units were becoming familiar, while electrical appliances and gadgets multiplied in number.

In terms of interior design, the decade saw major changes. There was a revival of interest in the use of colour, a growing interest in historic revivals, the rise of DIY, and the use of imagery from fine art, asymmetric shapes and motifs based on organic, atomic and parabolic originals. There was also a change in emphasis in International Style architecture, from meeting social needs to feeding corporate needs, and this embraced a new practice of office space planning. In addition, there was an increase in designers specialising in commercial furniture. The influence of these developments was to encourage the widespread use of a range of features including indoor plants, built-in furniture, venetian blinds, open storage cabinets, hard floors with skins and rugs, and textured brick and stone, all contrasting with soft upholstery and organic seating forms.

These changes exposed the indifference to the rational design approach of the Modernists in favour of an emotionally led one, which itself is reflected in considerations of choice, personality and individuality. The development of the personalisation of interiors fuelled further changes in the way that people related to their homes in order to overcome the alienation that much of modern life created. The rise of DIY decorating and home furnishing, for example, equated to a greater degree of control and personal achievement over one's interior, and perhaps reflected a sense of self-identity. This appropriation and control of the environment, and the achievement and expression of self, are not only satisfying in their own right, but indicate a degree of resistance and opposition to ready-made concepts of the imposed "ideal".

During the 1950s in Europe, there was a radical change in ideas concerning office layout. The German management consultants Quickborner developed the idea of a *Bürolandschaft* or "office-landscape". Rather than treat workers as part of a Taylorist "scientific management" system of production control, this plan considered people as

individuals through a sociological examination of human relations at work. The plan thus allowed for some freedom in the layout of furniture in large open-plan spaces. Although it used similar mechanical services to American examples, the employment of moveable partitions and organic planting created a degree of delineation and privacy. The use of fitted carpets and noise-absorbing ceiling panels also partially tempered the sounds of a large office. The benefit of this layout was the acknowledgement that office work was very wide-ranging, requiring a flexible approach to its planning and execution. Designers developed this further in the new non-hierarchical approach to office planning.

## USA

An interesting exhibition entitled What is Modern Interior Design? was set up by the Museum of Modern Art in New York, curated by Edgar Kaufmann Jr in 1953. He described interior design as "the art of arranging objects for agreeable living". More seriously, he defined the "new" traits of modern rooms as being "comfort, quality, lightness and harmony". A book, published to coincide with the exhibition, traces a well-known trajectory from William Morris and earlier, through the European Modernists to contemporary designers such as Charles Eames, Alexander Girard and Florence Knoll. Kaufmann finishes his train of development with two of Frank Lloyd Wright's works, which he sees as a contrast to the established machine aesthetic and the International Style because they link technology and nature seemingly in harmony.

In terms of American architecture and interiors, there were a number of other important developments. Frank Lloyd Wright's final masterpiece, the 1959 New York Guggenheim Museum, was an idiosyncratic and deeply personal examination of the museum interior, which not only expressed his organic credentials but also introduced the visitor to a continual spiral of exhibition space. In a somewhat similar vein was the TWA airport terminal, again in New York. Designed by Eero Saarinen and built between 1956 and 1962, it was an example of a total work of art with its architecture, interiors and accessories integrated through one eye.

Other smaller-scale projects include Edward Durell Stone's work of 1958 in the Bruno Graf house in Houston, featuring a dining area made from a disc of polished white marble that appears to float on water in the middle of the room; Philip Johnson and William Pahlmann's work on the famous Four Seasons Restaurant in the 1958 Seagram building where the entire decor was changed to match the season and the extravagant Neo-Baroque designs of Morris Lapidus for luxury Miami hotels including the 1954 Fontainebleau and the 1957 Eden Roc hotels. All of these clearly ran against the grain of mainstream Modernism, demonstrating the eclecticism to be found in any decade.

In the 1950s and '60s, the International Style skyscraper, or hermetically sealed "glass boxes", became the symbol of commercial and cultural success. With the development of successful air-conditioning and fluorescent lighting, these buildings could be laid out in any way required. There was no need to have natural lighting or ventilation, since the suspended ceilings allowed for artificial lighting and air supply. Interior design firms

such as the Knoll Planning Unit epitomized the elegantly furnished interiors, complete with collections of artworks. In fact, Florence Knoll spurred on the change from interior decorator to interior designer, whereby the designer became responsible for the space planning, services and equipment, as well as the furnishing and fittings and aesthetic input. Commercial interior design became bigger business, as work, environment and the brand or public face of companies become even more important. Architectural practices began to consider these aspects more, and firms such as Skidmore, Owings & Merrill and the Knoll Planning Unit took the lead in this work.

Florence Knoll Bassett was an American furniture designer and architect who trained in the Miesian Modernist tradition. She and Hans Knoll founded Knoll Associates to develop ranges of architect-designed furniture. Although she designed furniture in a strict Modernist style, it was her work for corporate offices that best demonstrated her American interpretation of the International Style's rationalist design theories. She applied the principles of design to solving space problems. Her ideal office had a fresh, orderly interior, based on open-plan layouts, in conjunction with iconic Modernist designers' furniture.

The growth of so-called "contract interiors" developed in this decade, a particular dedicated sector of interior work that specialized in furnishing and equipping offices. The corporate style of the decade was the large glass box multi-storey building with open-plan work stations, suspended ceilings, air conditioning and interior partitions.

## SCANDINAVIA

**RIGHT**
*The living room in the House of the Future, by Alison and Peter Smithson, 1956. The room – which was made of plastics and included many innovative futuristic features that have become familiar now – was in a showhouse exhibited at the Daily Mail Ideal Home Show in London.*

During the 1950s post-war period in particular, Scandinavian design reached wider popularity in the home-furnishings market. As a style it provided inspiration to many mass-production furniture designers in the USA and it established a furniture aesthetic that fashion-conscious consumers embraced most enthusiastically. Whether called Danish Modern, Swedish Modern or Scandinavian Modern, the style became familiar to many American and European families who lived with it throughout the 1950s to 1970s. It was no coincidence that the Scandinavian ideal became quickly recognized: it often reflected the "good design" characteristics defined by the then current thinking.

The international exhibition H55 held in the Swedish town of Helsingborg in 1955 was based on the idea of being a cultural rather than a trade fair, with an emphasis on arts and crafts. It was intended to show how modern design could be incorporated into regular goods, as well as luxury items. In North America, the Design in Sweden exhibition shown in various locations between 1954 and 1957 developed a widespread taste for interior furnishings in a "Scandinavian" style. The approach was essentially craft-based and human-centred, which was clearly attractive to many North Americans who were living with the uncertainties of the Cold War and the growth in technology and mass communications.

## BRITAIN

In Britain, the major event that was to influence the first part of the decade was the 1951 Festival of Britain. In terms of interiors, the stimulus was found in the furnishings and decorations of the Festival buildings themselves, and later on in the impact of the work of the designers and their products. These included surface designs from the Festival Pattern Group, the chairs of Ernest Race and the textile designs, especially the famous Calyx pattern, by Lucienne Day. The exhibition itself had a series of room settings planned by the Council of Industrial Design (CoID) all typifying the contemporary style, while the Festival Hall itself was avowedly modern. Throughout the exhibition interesting distinctions were made between a version of Modernism influenced by America and a self-indulgent and whimsical approach to design, which was very English.

In the UK, reformers who wanted to introduce modern design into the domestic sphere continued to influence post-war homes. The CoID (later the Design Council) was a key player in this development and sponsored many exhibitions, such as the examples seen at Hatfield New Town from 1953, which included a Modernist-influenced approach, where more traditional accessories enhanced simple contemporary furnishings. In 1956 the CoID opened the Design Centre in London, which was a showcase for 'approved' designs for homes and business products.

In some contrast, the annual Ideal Home Exhibition, sponsored by the *Daily Mail* newspaper, offered a counter-culture which displayed a range of interior products including furnished show houses, reproduction furniture and DIY project materials. The show encouraged the purchase of domestic equipment, for kitchens in particular. One of the most interesting displays was Alison and Peter Smithson's "House of the Future" in the 1956 show. The house was certainly of the future: it was made from moulded plastic and intended to be upgraded or even disposed of when out of fashion. Unlike the permanence of the Modernists, it reflected the popular culture of style changes that were found in fashion and automobile design of the period. Clustered round a central space with hi-tech fittings and details such as tables rising from the floor and disposable plastic furniture, it was a clear challenge to tradition. Nevertheless, for most of the annual exhibitions, traditional show houses and furnishings were the most popular.

It was this decade that saw a new wave of British consumers who were influenced by a range of external cultural images including American popular culture and Italian "espresso" style. The influence on interiors of a wide variety of visual cultures was to become even more potent in this decade. This development was particularly noticeable in the design of boutique shops in the retail sector. Mary Quant opened her Bazaar store on the King's Road in 1955, and in 1957 moved to a new store designed by Terence Conran. This was the beginning of a major change in retail interior design, where the spaces and the atmosphere were exciting in themselves and were in competition, to a degree, with the merchandise.

In some contrast to these trends was the work of more upmarket British designers, who were confidently mixing and matching to create eclectic but distinctive and inspiring interiors. Designers such as Michael Inchbald and David Hicks were in the vanguard of this development. In 1953, *House and Garden* featured Hicks's boldly coloured rooms created in his mother's house. This set him on a path where he was to be a major player in the 1960s and 1970s in the high fashion world of celebrity interior design. Inchbald, a society designer, decreed interior design to be "not simply a matter of colour, it is more a matter of eye, line and proportion. Get that right and the rest will follow."

John Fowler and his ideals of a faded English country house as a version of romantic Englishness also began to coalesce in this decade. His partnership with American tastemaker Nancy Lancaster, who bought the firm of Colefax & Co. in the 1940s, was to develop into one of the most successful companies, and styles, of the century under the name of Colefax and Fowler. Their success in furnishing country houses in particular was in their ability to mix formality with comfort, and elegance with flamboyance, which allowed for a revised approach to interiors. Fowler, who called himself an architectural decorator was a consummate craftsman with a wide knowledge of historic styles, which aided him in the recreation of the English country house style for private clients and bodies such as the National Trust.

The revival of a British academic interest in Victorian art and design was symbolized

**ABOVE**
*Living room by E. H. Martin, 1950.* The focal point of this eclectic room is the monochrome tiling artwork, but the standard lamp and coffee table are also noteworthy for their design.

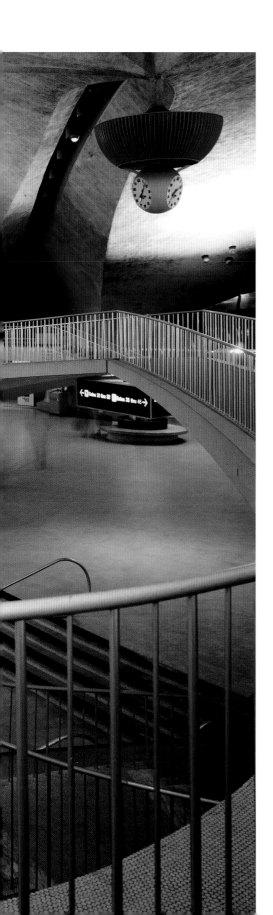

**LEFT**
*TWA Terminal, New York, by Eero Saarinen, 1956-62.*
*The organic-designed interior of the terminal was planned so that all the elements would appear to be a continuous ribbon linking the exterior, ceilings and walls and those walls with floors and back again.*

**BELOW**
*A corridor in l'Unité d'Habitation, Marseilles, by Le Corbusier, 1952.*
*The corridor with its sets of variously coloured doors reflects both the concept of a passageway on an ocean liner and the individualized entrances to each flat rather like a street.*

**RIGHT**
*Overview of the House of the Future by Alison and Peter Smithson, 1956.*
The central garden patio is surrounded by pavilion that had honey-coloured plastic skin paneling, stretched over all the walls, floors and ceilings.

by the 1952 Victoria and Albert Museum exhibition, *Victorian and Edwardian Decorative Arts*. This sowed the seeds of a greater awareness of historic materials and products, a taste for mixing and matching and a more irreverent approach to interior design than the official line from the Council of Industrial Design.

## FRANCE

In France, the decade also had a number of varied contrasting styes, including the work of Le Corbusier, Jean Prouvé, Madeleine Castaing and Maison Jansen. Le Corbusier, the arch-Modernist, put his ideas for living into practice in his Unité d'Habitation development in Marseilles. Here his ideas of town planning matched his interior architecture. Double-height rooms, open-plan spaces, along with living balconies, allowed the best use of the light and air of southern France. His Maisons Jaoul, two adjoining small houses with vaulted ceilings, exposed brick work and concrete, with interior finishes of natural materials such as wood, and tile, contrasted with the brightly painted wall surfaces.

In stark contrast to the modernism of Corbusier was the work of the decorator Madeleine Castaing. She has been called the "decorators' decorator" and with good reason. She said: "Don't be intimidated by audacity. Be audacious – but with unusual taste." Her interior designs were both exuberant and colourful. She developed a particular approach that was at once bold, exciting and witty. An example of this was her juxtaposition of combinations of Victorian, Napoleon III, gilded Russian and Swedish furniture with sumptuous swag curtains, exotically patterned carpets, vibrant Majolica, and esoteric accessories. This eclectic but witty approach was rather ahead of its time, but is now widely appreciated as an exciting contribution to interior decoration.

A further final contrast to Modernist approaches was the continuing work of Maison Jansen. The firm's principal, Stéphane Boudin, was well known for his *tous les Louis* approach. The firm undertook interior design work for the Duke and Duchess of Windsor: firstly in their Paris house, then, after the war, at the Moulin de la Tuilerie, and finally in their house in the Bois de Boulogne. The interiors were, not surprisingly, a clever amalgam of British royal palace design and American brashness.

The interior design of this decade reflected not only a revision of Modernism but also an embracement of pluralism aided by the growth in visual media and culture. The rise of the corporate market was an important factor in post-war developments in interior design. It resulted in people making distinctions between those who worked as space planners and interior designers, and those whose work mainly concentrated on the domestic, as stylists or interior decorators.

**ABOVE**

*A living space by G. Pons, 1950.*
*The area is divided by a curtain to separate the two required functions of the space.*

**RIGHT**

*A living room by A. Pinsard, 1950.*
*Furnished with a Saarinen Womb chair and a particularly esoteric treatment of the fireplace, a vertical blind separates the two areas when closed.*

**LEFT**
*Bedroom for a young man, 1950.*
*This stylised interior has a*
*light oak sideboard and a*
*divan that can be converted*
*into a bed for the night.*

**ABOVE**
*Large living room by Belluschi,
1950*. The enormous
geometric fireplace creates
an axis, whilst the more
organic furniture softens the
look of the space.

**RIGHT**
*Living room in designer's own
house, Grosse Pointe, Michigan,
by Alexander Girard, 1950.* In
this pine-beamed living
room a curved screen
divides the studio from the
living area. The built-in
furniture and seating in
dark brown with red and
yellow cushions sits on a
grey concrete floor.

**ABOVE**

*Sitting room in Mrs Herman Kiaer's house, by William Platt and Joseph Mullen, 1950.* The pine panelling is an unusual backdrop for the modern furniture and art works. The pineapple design on the chairs create an interesting contrast.

**RIGHT**

*Living room by Jean Royère, 1950.*

The yellow check Scottish tweed upholstery contrasts with the marble floor and oriental rugs. The table and lamp are of forged iron and bronze.

**BELOW RIGHT**

*Living room by Jean Royère, 1950.*

The sycamore furniture is off-set by antique rose satin coverings and maroon worsted drapery with hanging lights of gilt forged iron.

**FAR RIGHT**

*An electric brazier, by Berry's Electric Magical, 1950s.*

Apparently this period style electric 'glowing coal' brazier could be successfully used in a modern setting.

**OPPOSITE**

*Children's recreation room in USA, by Twitchell & Rudolph, 1950.*

The wall and ceiling of this playroom are of umber and grey cypress harmonizing with the Italian rose marble flooring.

**RIGHT**

*Interior view from the living room towards the balcony, in the Eames House, Pacific Palisades, California, August 1950.* The house was part of the Case Study House Program, sponsored by Art & Architecture magazine, in which a number of architects were commissioned to design post-World War II homes that specifically addressed the needs of the prospective inhabitants.

**OPPOSITE**

*Open-plan sitting room, c. 1950.* The room is divided by shelves – on one side, the living and dining rooms, on the other, the office and library.

**ABOVE**

*Bedroom for a young girl by Jean Royère, 1950*. The furniture in the room is lacquered metal with pale yellow fabric covered in orange and mauve flowers.

**ABOVE**
*A small apartment by Jean Prouvé and Charlotte Perriand, 1950.*
*This room shows Perriand's bookcase design and a large built-in cupboard on the right with aluminium doors.*

**OPPOSITE**
*A salon by J. Dumond, 1950.* The room has brightly coloured banquette cushions, a floor paved with Comblanchien limestone, and an arresting upholstery fabric design.

**BELOW**
**Drawing room in a cottage, France, 1950.**
*The room is furnished in a modern blue colour scheme that contrasts with the cottage architecture.*

**ABOVE**
*Living room, Sweden, 1950s.*
An example of the interior
of an ordinary Swedish
flat complete with typical
furnishings.

**RIGHT**
*A bedroom, Canada, by R. Simon, 1950.* The scheme here includes grey furnishings and
a fine rayon curtain around
the raised plinth bed.

**LEFT**

*A drawing room/salon by
H. Pottier, 1950.* The walls of
white stone in this room
contrast with a slate floor
and a sofa with yellow and
orange cushions.

**LEFT**

*Living space, France, by
L. Mirabaud, 1950.* A scheme
of red and white with various furnishings including
small squares of latex foam
covered in felt for seating.

**RIGHT**
*A living room by M. Mategot,
1950.* The black lacquered
iron furniture with rat-
tan covers in this room
contrasts with the lilac wall
finish. Notice the unusual
storage cabinet.

**RIGHT**
*A bathroom display, 1951.*
A comfortable bathroom
fitted with a grey Formica
counter, a blue washbasin
and a dark grey leatherette
frontage.

**LEFT**
*Dining room, c. 1950s.* This tasteful dining room shows the influence of Danish design on wooden furniture of the 1950s.

**LEFT**
*American kitchen designed by William Snaith, 1951.*
Most of the products on view were designed by the studios of Raymond Loewy Associates. An example of the aspirational kitchen of the 1950s.

**RIGHT**
***Interior furnished by Liberty and Co. London, 1951.*** *A typical British contemporary look with furniture by Ercol and HK and lamps by Merchant Adventurers, with imported birch wall desk.*

**LEFT**

*Antelope chairs by Ernest Race, 1951.* This view of part of the 1951 Festival of Britain shows the Antelope chair in a bar with pot plants and a room divider.

**BELOW**

*Albergo Nuova Italia by Jacopini Osvaldo, 1951.* This Italian hotel interior shows a range of contemporary furnishings that were ultra-modern at the time.

**OVERLEAF**

*Farnsworth House, Plano, Illinois, by Mies van der Rohe, 1951.* The house is one of the best expressions of Modernist ideals in its striving for perfection in design.

**RIGHT**
*Calyx design fabric by Lucienne Day for Heals, London, 1951.*
A ground-breaking fabric design used in the Festival of Britain contemporary design displays.

**OPPOSITE**
*Rig design fabric by Lucienne Day for Heals, London, 1953.* A typical screen-printed linen fabric design intended to harmonise with contemporary lightweight furniture styles.

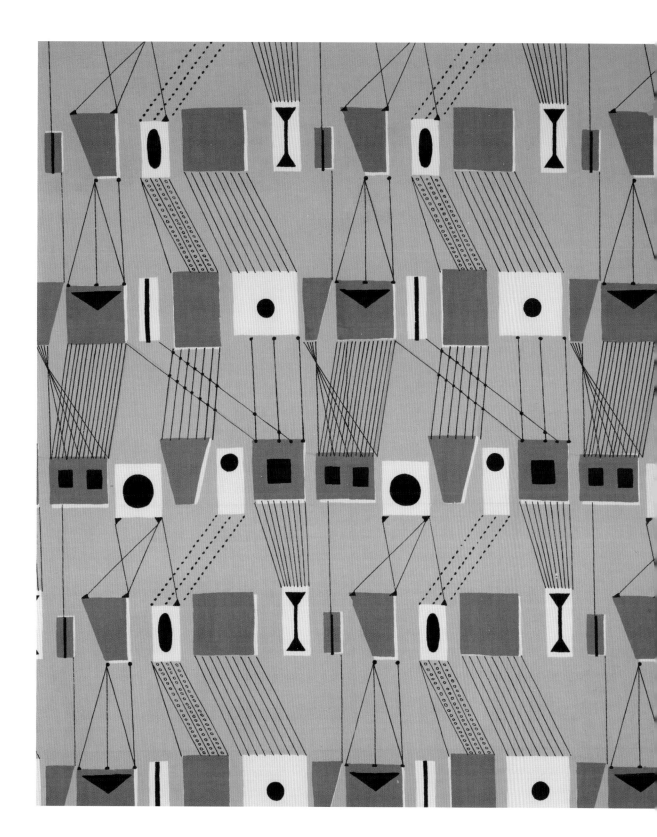

**ABOVE**
*Schrafft's food bar, Chrysler Building, New York, 1953*. An example of a 'quick service lunch' restaurant, the fore-runner of fast-food outlets.

**ABOVE**
*Living room by Pierre Guariche,*
*France, 1953.* Typical features
of the period are evident in
the spindly furniture legs,
Venetian blinds, pot plants
and simple shelving system.

**ABOVE**
*A living room in a modern French family apartment, 1953.* These flats in France were specifically rent controlled and known as HLM (habitation à loyer modéré).

**RIGHT**
*A living room designed by Frederick Manning, 1953.* The greyish-yellow brick of the exposed chimney breast dictates the green, grey and mustard colour scheme. The settee breaks up into separate chairs if required.

**LEFT**

*A living room in a small modern house, 1953.* This drawing is typical of many illustrated works that showed readers renderings of interiors furnished in up-to-the-minute styles.

**LEFT**

*A living room decor suggestion, by Kelvin MacAvoy, 1953.* "The sharp, clean colours of the parti-coloured walls, the delicate lines of the furniture and modern storage unit, all speak of tomorrow".

**ABOVE**

*Heal and Son stand, Ideal Home Exhibition, Olympia, London, 1953.* This popular exhibition allowed the public to see the latest in home furnishings.

**OPPOSITE**

*Office in the Price Tower, Bartlesville, Oklahoma, by Frank Lloyd Wright, 1953–56.* The continual re-invention of his architectural practice is evident in the building and in the aluminium furniture.

**RIGHT AND BELOW RIGHT**
*Kronish House in Beverly Hills, by Richard Neutra, 1955.*
Neutra moved Modernism away from concrete and white walls to a more 'contemporary' use of natural materials for floors and cladding. Clean lines combined with these materials reduced the sterility of earlier Modernism.

**OPPOSITE**
*Kronish House in Beverly Hills, by Richard Neutra, 1955.* Neutra's ideas about free flowing space, derived from an interest in Japan, glass walls to enclose and a stress on function are evident in this view of the interior.

**ABOVE**

*A room setting by Louis Sognot
and Maurice Rinck, France,
1956.* The room features
contemporary art works on
the chimney breast and in
the wall hanging.

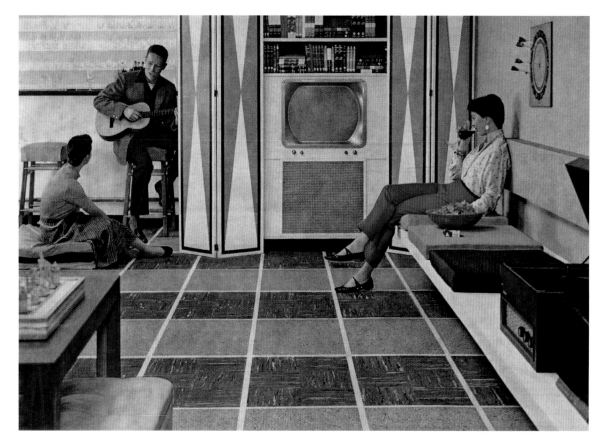

**ABOVE**
**American advert for Kentile tile flooring, 1956.** *The interest and promotion of DIY was a feature during this period.*

**OVERLEAF**
**Congresso Nacional do Brasil (National Congress of Brazil) by Oscar Niemeyer, 1958.** *This shows a rather surreal interior space with tiles and planting within the Modernist concrete framing of the Congress building.*

**RIGHT**
*Image from advert for Formica, 1959.* The use of decorative laminates such as Formica in this period reflected a taste for easily maintained decorated surfaces and the growth of DIY practices.

**BELOW LEFT AND RIGHT**
*House in Tokyo, Japan, 1959.* Interconnecting ten-mat rooms based on the typical module of 2:1 with sliding screens and a transom grille in cypress wood lacquered dark brown.

**LEFT**
*A dining set by E. Gomme,
High Wycombe, 1959.* The
Rotadiner table in tola
wood on a black pedestal
base had a novel hidden
mechanism that allowed
the table to move to coffee
table height.

**LEFT**
*Dining room of the Trier
(Usonian) house, Johnston, Iowa,
designed by Frank Lloyd Wright,
c.1956.* Wright's interest in
small, easily run houses
(Usonian) was long stand-
ing. In this example we can
also see a set of laminated
chairs designed for this
house in the living/dining
room space.

# 1960–1969

After years of austerity in Britain and the West, there began a period of affluence during which old certainties began to erode and experiment and change were encouraged. The post-war youth explosion, imported products, increased foreign travel, attitudes derived from film and television, an engagement with technology, a revival of crafts and an interest in alternatives to contemporary Western lifestyles were all catalysts in this. The decade was one of plural approaches to design, as design thinking began to change from a Modernist-driven agenda to one more influenced by popular culture and social fluctuations.

Alongside these developments, some older beliefs remained, although they were often associated with a particular taste or age group. Modernism still had a following, as did some historic revivals and looser interpretations of past styles. However, interior design and design in general was not about Modernist ideals of morality, anti-historicism or abstraction during this period; rather it embraced concepts related to symbolism, metaphor, kitsch, pop and plastic. Design was high-style fashion, not truth; design was fun, not philosophy.

It was often architects who led the change. The Archigram group in London conveyed their frustration with Modernism in their 1961 manifesto; the Italian Archizoom group founded in 1966 had a similar mission in Italy and in America, Robert Venturi's 1966 book *Complexity and Contradiction in Architecture* heralded an eclectic and cosmopolitan approach to interiors that promoted individuality in spaces. The diktats of the apparent simplicity of pure Modernism had been relieved by an understanding that life was not straightforward and "pure" and therefore interiors should not reflect this.

In reality this approach had probably been going on for a long time in ordinary homes, where interiors grew and developed over the years. Nevertheless, the work of the radical architects and designers – that they themselves described as hybrid, distorted, ambiguous and interesting – laid the path for later post-Modernism and a full acceptance of difference within the profession. The domestic interiors of the 1960s demonstrate the approach with a stereotypical amalgam of contrasting materials, oversize lettering, antiques and bric-a-brac, mixed with modern furniture pieces, highlighted architectural detailing and amusing accessories. One place where Modernism was fully embraced was in corporate environments.

Although architects and interior designers had been working with commercial environments for many years, the concept of "contract design" for commercial and institutional spaces grew apace in the 1960s. During the decade, a new concept in office design challenged the tradition of partitioned individual rooms. American firms such as ISD, Design for Business and the Space Design group adopted the *Bürolandschaft*

**ABOVE**

*The No-stop City. Interior landscape by Archizoom, 1969.*

This anti-design group saw the urban experience as a continuous and relentless flow, thus repetition was reflected in their imagery.

concept, originally developed in Germany. The concept of the open office, fitted out with minimal low-level partitioning, required specially designed furniture and equipment. The Action office system, initially designed by Robert Propst, was based on a system of screens and panels developed by the Herman Miller Co. The idea was to create working cubicles by using two or three upright divisions that marked off a space territory: it offered privacy but also allowed visual access to the rest of the spaces.

## USA

In America these contrasting approaches can be seen in the range of interiors produced during the decade. The softening of Modernism in corporate building is demonstrated in Warren Platner's interior work in conjunction with architecture firm Roche Dinkeloo. He was praised for the interior design of the Ford Foundation headquarters, built in 1967. Here he combined a subdued but warm colour scheme with mahogany and bronze furniture, which contrasted somewhat with the steel and glass construction of the building itself.

In the same year, the Hyatt Regency hotel was opened in Atlanta. John Portman's achievement was to redefine the hotel interior, using a design approach that remained successful for many years. In this work, the grand lobbies of the 1920s hotels were reinvented. By arriving through a low-canopied entrance, the visitor then entered a full height (22-storey) atrium, complete with an enormous aviary, a 120-foot high sculpture and visible "bubble" elevators. Here a sensation and atmosphere was created that expressed something of the excitement of travel through glamorous surroundings. Even the rooms opened on to plant-lined balconies, rather than soulless corridors. His interiors delivered a sensory experience that was at odds with established ideals, though struck a chord with the public and influenced many other interior design projects.

The third contrasting example of organic design is the TWA airport terminal in New

**RIGHT**
*The Ford Foundation building, New York, by Kevin Roche and Warren Platner, 1967. These spaces represented a major difference from the typical office tower block. The designers produced an environment that was sympathetic to the goals of the foundation and where the individual worker or visitor could relate to them.*

**LEFT**
*The Ford Foundation building New York, 1967 by Kevin Roche and Warren Platner.* *The Corten steel, glass and granite building materials contrast with the central garden in this twelve-storey atrium of an iconic Modernist building. The focus on interior views of garden spaces was an important advance in office design at the time.*

York, designed by Eero Saarinen and opened in 1962. The building was notable for a number of interior design elements, not least that all the services and fittings were integral to the structure. Seating, signage, workstations and service columns are all incorporated into the sculptural forms that infuse the buildings. The overall effect is large and spacious and even serene, with an off-white and charcoal colour scheme, balanced by a deep-red waiting lounge pit. This was a great example of the total design concept that would become familiar in many later rebranding exercises.

Even more detailed was the work of Alexander Girard who designed every feature of

the New York *La Fonda del Sol* restaurant which opened in 1960. Using a Latin American modern theme, he used more than 80 different sun motifs throughout the restaurant interior, and graphic design work that demonstrated an exaggerated attempt at unifying an idea. The motif was used on all sorts of surfaces and represented in a variety of shapes and sizes using different imagery, clearly reflecting the restaurant's name. The clustered dining alcoves, each upholstered in beige or patterned fabric, and the seating with chairs covered to match, created a vibrant and exciting interior. His greatest achievement, however, is arguably his work for Braniff Airlines in 1965. For this company he designed the aircraft cabin interiors, the passenger lounges, furniture and graphics: everything down to the sugar packets.

Decorators continued to be successful personalities in their particular arena of work and often created "trademark looks". One such decorator was Billy Baldwin, who developed his signature coromandel black-brown high-gloss enamel paint and his highly adaptable Slipper chair, as well as popularizing the concept of working with pattern on pattern. The Parish Hadley company demonstrated their skills in the combining of contrasting patterns and colours on the one hand and a Modernist attention to spaces on the other, also undertaking restoration work on the White House.

The development of Modernism into a form of Minimalism in the USA was exemplified in particular by the works of Ward Bennett and Benjamin Baldwin. Their interiors were often composed of simple planes, a minimal colour palette, venetian blinds, luxurious furnishings and exclusive art work. These interiors were elegant and restrained, though without the political agendas associated with pre-war Modernism.

However, pre-war models were not shunned completely. The Knoll Company reissued a number of classic furniture items as well as developing their own range of Modernist designs, and for many corporate interiors variations of Modernism remained the norm.

## ITALY

In Italy during this decade, Milan became the hothouse of Italian invention in many aspects of design. Andrea Branzi and colleagues, who established Archizoom in 1966, were particularly antagonistic towards the idea of "elegant design" being used as a status symbol while ignoring popular cultural imagery. Their approach created designs that were intended to be subversive and anti-functional. For example, the flat elastic seat of the Mies chair, designed for Poltronova in 1969, demonstrates this radical and challenging approach by mocking "classic" design in a very unorthodox manner. At the same time, there was a growing taste for iconic furniture of the 1920s and 1930s, and therefore furniture companies – Gavina and Cassina, among others – produced reproductions of classic Modernist furniture by Breuer, Le Corbusier and Charlotte Perriand that often sat quite comfortably in a wide variety of interiors.

The artist and architect Joe Colombo developed an interest in interiors in the 1960s. Soon after his office was established in 1961, he received awards for his interior work in the Hotel Pontinental in Sardinia. Although his designs for plastic furniture are most well known, his mobile structures, which combined to make a complete environment, were also very interesting. His habitation units or pods were based on modules: "kitchen", "cupboard", "bed and privacy" and "bathroom". They offered a space-age vision of practical living that could be mass-produced to be both functional and futuristic.

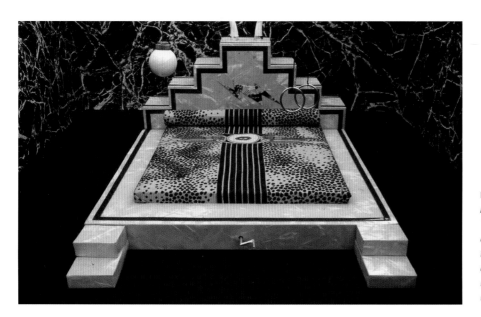

**LEFT**
*Dream bed by Archizoom, Italy, 1967.* These monumentally designed beds that quoted from a range of historic art and design references were intended as a challenge to bourgeois society.

**ABOVE**

*Central Living Block, designed by Joe Colombo, 1969.* The 'central living unit', part of Colombo's complete home or 'total functioning unit' was intended for daily activities such as reading and listening to music. An integrated television and shelving unit is suspended above the seating area.

## SCANDINAVIA

Although Scandinavian design was still popular at a grass-roots level, with teak-veneered cabinet furniture, wooden-framed upholstery and machine-made rya rugs, the post-war taste for its ideals had begun to decline in avant-garde circles in favour of Italian and American styles. Nevertheless, the successful amalgam of craft and machine that produced a comfortable, human but slightly boring interior remained a model for many years to come in the mainstream of popular taste.

A notable designer who represented different aspects of Danish design, was Arne Jacobsen. Influenced by the Bauhaus and Gunnar Asplund, he was already a successful architect and designer in a Modern idiom. In 1960 Jacobsen won the commission to design St Catherine's College, Oxford. Like others before him, he insisted on designing not only the building but also the interior, its fixtures, fittings and even the garden. It is a fine example of a self-disciplined, beautifully detailed Modernist interior scheme. In contrast to this was his SAS Royal Hotel, opened in Copenhagen in 1960, which again showcased his desire to create a complete building as a work of art, the vision of one man, but which in this case put organic garden-themed interiors with a Modernist glass box exterior. The famous Egg and Swan chairs demonstrate an organic theme in both interiors.

**LEFT**
*St. Catherine's College, Oxford University, by Arne Jacobsen, 1962.* The plan of the complex is based on a reinterpretation of the established "Oxbridge" quad. Arne Jacobsen pursued a restrained Modernist approach in his design that included most aspects of the architectural shell and the interior.

**LEFT**
*St. Catherine's College library, Oxford University, by Arne Jacobsen, 1962.* The Danish architect designed the interior fittings, lighting and accessories including the chairs in the library of the College.

Different again was the work of another Dane named Verner Panton. An all-round designer, he rose to prominence in the 1960s with designs for furniture, textiles and lighting. "Most people spend their lives living in dreary, beige conformity, mortally afraid of using colours," he said. "The main purpose of my work is to provoke people into using their imagination and make their surroundings more exciting." In 1969 his upholstered units called Living Towers were first displayed as examples of a so-called living landscape. The ultimate example of his living landscape concept was Panton's exhibition *Visiona II* presented at the Cologne Furniture Fair of 1970. It was a fantastic organic design of a red and blue cave-like interior that seemed to reflect a psychedelic image, which was so appropriate as a statement of the end of a decade of excess. The exhibit was actually intended to sell Bayer's new Dralon textile, but succeeded in becoming a major icon of the 1960s in itself.

The decade saw the rise of the Space Age, peaking in 1969 with the delivery of a man on the moon. This event and the general interest in space and technology encouraged another strand of interior design: the concept of capsule living was generally an idiosyncratic ideal, rarely realized, but the use of space age imagery was popular. Whether it was rockets printed on textiles, white plastic globular-shaped furniture or lamps, or even silver-coloured stainless steel and glass, the connections with modern technology and science were inescapable.

French designer Olivier Mourgue linked a number of contemporary ideas in his chairs used in the film *2001: A Space Odyssey* (1968). The amoeba-like Djinn furniture covered with stretch fabric in bright colours that furnished the space hotel was offset by all-white high tech interior spaces. Both features expressed two of the major styles of the decade.

**OPPOSITE**
*A showroom featuring furniture and lighting designs by Verner Panton, c.1969. The bright colours and unadorned simple shapes reflected a complete change in approaches to design at the time.*

**BELOW**
*The rotating Hilton Hotel featured in the film 2001: A Space Odyssey, by Stanley Kubrick, 1968. The Djinn chairs designed by Olivier Mourgue in 1965 featured in the hotel lobby scenes.*

## BRITAIN

In the United Kingdom, a number of cultural developments came together to inject the art and design scene with a new and youthful approach. London, for much of the period, became the centre for fashion, graphics, interiors and accessories. Fuelled by the work of the Independent Group, the Op Art painters and the Pop Art movement, young designers saw a new way of thinking about all aspects of art and design. Richard Hamilton's prescient 1957 definition of Pop Art, which proclaimed it as "popular, transient, expendable, low-cost, mass-produced, young, witty, sexy, gimmicky, glamorous, and Big Business" was fully validated in the 1960s.

Expendability and pluralism allowed for some new expression of identity that had been missing in prescribed approaches to interiors. Designers adopted the Pop aesthetic in popular commercial locations such as restaurants and boutique shops and in domestic products, including wallpaper, textiles and furniture. In addition, Pop design avoided the dictatorial approaches of Modernism and instead embraced variety, difference and attitude. This approach recognized a pluralistic society which did not want to have a particular set of values or ruling tastes imposed upon it. This

**RIGHT**
*Living room by David Hicks for John Panchaud, 1960s. The signature geometric carpet design is evident, as is the balanced aysymmetry of the design scheme and layout.*

youth-orientated market therefore embraced imagery from Art Nouveau, Victoriana, popular culture and American film and music, as well as art movements. Colour and pattern reigned supreme. Whether it was DayGlo tints and environments designed to be "experienced", or reworked and re-coloured versions of William Morris patterns for the less adventurous, Pop interiors were intended to be expressive of the new mood.

While this pop approach was revitalizing parts of the interior design world, another equally radical approach to up-market design work was being offered by the designer David Hicks. He established himself in the late 1950s using a very particular approach that combined antique and modern furniture, and bold colour schemes set off by abstract paintings, often in interesting architectural spaces. In 1968 he said in his publication *Living with Taste*: "My greatest contribution as an interior designer has been to show people how to use bold colour mixtures, how to use patterned carpets, how to light rooms and how to mix old with new." One minor but particular contribution to interior design was his establishment of the "tablescape" (a pleasing arrangement of objects carefully selected and laid out with an artist eye onto a table top) as a minor art practice.

In the more rarefied world of country house interiors, John Fowler's work with the National Trust continued a trend towards revision and conservation of historic houses that still influences today's thinking. The "country house look" and its apparent eclecticism filtered down to other less glamorous interiors, which also encouraged a – still fashionable today – taste for architectural salvage, bric-a-brac and antique hunting.

The death of Le Corbusier in 1965 and Walter Gropius and Mies van der Rohe in 1969 symbolically heralded the end of a particular version of Modernism that was already challenged on many fronts. Although the anti-design and radical design movements challenged old ways of thinking about interiors and products, much of their work remained rarefied and exclusive. In contrast, there arose a craft revival which rejected the expendable disposable ethos of the Pop design world in favour of a more conscious understanding of society and the environment. Companies like Habitat in the UK, Crate & Barrel in the USA and IKEA in Sweden offered good simple furnishings and home products based on a number of stylistic tendencies that included a reformed Modernism, a farmhouse style and watered-down pop imagery – any of which could define an individual lifestyle. Indeed these types of businesses returned to the display of merchandise in "lifestyle vignettes", which showed groups of objects in loose room settings so that the display would encourage the purchase of a ready-made lifestyle. For both merchandisers and customers the idea of "lifestyle" was to dominate the 1970s.

**LEFT**
*Architect's own house at Lauttasaari, Finland, by Toivo Korhonen, 1960.* The dining/living/library spaces of this architect-designed house run continuously as a gallery along the courtyard.

**RIGHT**

*Dragon Rock House, New York State, by Russel Wright, 1961.* Russel Wright was an industrial designer well known for ceramics. The two level living room features an angled sofa with changeable upholstery, and a wall of textured dark green plaster embedded with hemlock needles.

**RIGHT**

*Dragon Rock House, New York State, by Russel Wright, 1961.* The living room fireplace demonstrates the concept of using local material to blend the house with nature.

**OPPOSITE**

*Detail of fireplace in Stockholm apartment, 1961.* This apartment planned by textile designer Astrid Sampe shows the special atmosphere that a fireside can create.

**ABOVE**

*Helena Rubenstein's London flat by David Hicks, 1961.* A riot of bold colours, a hallmark of the designer, are found in this room. The walls are of purple silk, the American 19th century furniture is covered in magenta and purple felt, with a blond oak floor and gilded brass supports for displays.

**ABOVE**
*Dining room by David Hicks, 1960s*. This room shows Hicks's remarkable talent for dramatic colour schemes as well as his trademark geometric repeat carpet designs.

**OPPOSITE**
*An interior in 'Swedish blond' style, with furniture by Carl Malmsten, 1962. Malmsten was an advocate of traditional Swedish craftsmanship, with his designs often being inspired by examples from the Swedish vernacular. Here, the muted colours of brown, green and yellow offset the pine furniture, as do the crafted textiles.*

**ABOVE**
*Bachelor's apartment in Copenhagen, c.1962. A complete living space in a very small area has a 'floating' couch in natural linen, with orange, red and magenta cushions all set off by a black carpet and white walls.*

**PREVIOUS PAGE**
*Case Study House No. 25, Long Beach, California, 1962.*
*The Case Study Houses were trials supported by Art and Architecture magazine to design and build economical and efficient model homes for the United States post war housing needs. This house designed by Brady, Killingsworth & Smith on the Rivo Alto Canal shows an unusual tall front door and internal courtyard with the two living levels visible on the left.*

**ABOVE**
*Villa in Karuizawa, Japan, by Ichigaya office, 1960s.* This view of a holiday home shows the living space with sunken hearth and the traditional stove for the tea ceremony in the centre.

**OPPOSITE**
*Villa near Tokyo by Ichigaya office, 1962.* This view shows the 'Irori' room with sunken hearth and the traditional stove for the tea ceremony in the centre. The cedar beams and roof linings make a connection with the surrounding woodlands.

**OPPOSITE**
*Kitchen in HM residence, Japan, by Nakajima & Assocs, c. 1965.* The space is divided from the dining area by a partial timber wall on the left. The open display of crockery creates visual interest, as does the frieze effect above.

**LEFT**
*Apartment by Jean Royère, Paris, 1962.* This living room has a violet carpet, pearl grey upholstery, white walls and sycamore cabinets inset with yellow fabric. The tapestry is by Picart Le Doux.

**BELOW**
*Room in house in Dusseldorf by Paul Schneider-Esleben, 1962.* The black and white colour scheme is slightly relieved by teak bookcases either side of the fireplace.

**RIGHT**

*The Red Room in the White House, Washington, designed by Stéphane Boudin of Maison Jansen, 1962.* The traditional interior decorating company furnished the room mainly in the American Federal style using many antique pieces by the French émigré cabinetmaker Charles-Honoré Lannuier.

**RIGHT**

*The Blue Room in the White House, Washington, designed by Stéphane Boudin of Maison Jansen, 1962.* The oval shaped room was restored by Jansen under the Kennedy administration which returned several original Monroe-era chairs designed by Pierre-Antoine Bellangé. Reproductions of the Monroe armchairs and side chairs were made by Maison Jansen. The rectangular antique carpet is a Savonnerie product.

**LEFT**

*Wallpaper design, 1962.* A Persian inspired wallpaper design in the fashionable gold/black and brown colourway. The polystyrene ceiling was painted gold and the cushions were covered in bright blue fabric.

**LEFT**

*Apartment in Camden Town London, by John Donat, c.1962.* One wall of the apartment has a modular storage system based on the size of groups of books. The units are directly attached to the brick wall. The kelim rug adds colour and texture to the room.

**OVERLEAF**

*G plan furniture room set, England, 1963.* A setting showing a white finished table and chairs, convertible sofa and a sideboard reflecting commercial responses to Danish modern design.

**ABOVE**

*Chairs suspended from the ceiling, 1964.* An amusing idea by designer Verner Panton to aid housekeeping by avoiding furniture legs cluttering up the floor.

**OPPOSITE**

*A 'boom room' with armchairs of lacquered wood, 1965.* The chairs have removable cotton covers whilst the three-tier revolving book-case in Oregon pine reflects the taste for pine furniture. The ubiquitous rubber plant features prominently.

**RIGHT**

*Villa Aarnio, Kuusisaari,
Finland by Toivo Korhonen,
1966*. The living room of
this reinforced concrete
house shows the use of
white painted concrete as
a divider and storage unit
combined.

**RIGHT**

*Seating and wall units in the
Summa furniture range, Terence
Conran, 1966*. Terence Conran's intervention into the
design of furniture, interiors
and accessories was a
milestone in the develop-
ment of a new approach to
design which engaged with
a youthful market.

*Villa Aarnio, Kuusisaari, Finland by Toivo Korhonen, 1966.* The view to the hall showing how the architectural details create decorative effects.

**RIGHT**
*Double A cottage, Trent Canal,
Ontario, by Leo Venchiarutti,
1966.* This all wood- Canadian holiday cottage uses
the A-frame design to the
best advantage of the lake
view and also for maximum
sunlight penetration.

**RIGHT**
*Town House and Studio, Lower
Manhattan, New York, by Helmut
Jacoby, 1966.* The living
area of a small but flexible
space in New York featuring
classic Modernist furniture
and features including
simple elegant lines, natural
surfaces and a display of a
major art work.

**ABOVE**
*Living room in a residence in Toronto, by J. C. Parkin, 1966.*
*A general view of the living room of the residence showing the fireplace as a focal point with four iconic Barcelona chairs ranged on either side.*

*Verner Panton's "Phantasy Land-scape" 1968.* The use of colour and form in this psychedelic maze of tunnels, cavities, and interconnecting spaces established this setting as a paradigm of Pop design. This exhibition piece was intended to consider the idea of experiential interior spaces.

**OPPOSITE**

*The kitchen in the Miller House, Lakeville, Connecticut, by Peter Eisenman, 1969-70.* This view shows the internal deconstructivist geometry of the building through the white abstract rectilinear shapes that dominate the spaces.

**ABOVE**

*Concept design for a NASA stateroom in a space station, Raymond Loewy, 1968.*

This drawing by consultant designer Loewy and his studio shows an astronaut sitting at a desk with pull-out seat, using a phone in a general area within a tube-like spaceship frame.

**ABOVE**
*A 1960s living room.*
*This room features many of
the typical furnishings of a
mid-range modern interior
of the 1960s. The potted
plants, pleated lampshades
and Danish inspired furniture are all representative of
contemporary taste.*

**ABOVE**
*Fitted kitchen/diner, 1960s.*
*A woman stands in her modern fitted kitchen that features a tiled floor, lots of storage space and work surfaces, modern equipment and a small dining area on the left.*

**RIGHT**

*A display of one of the most iconic chairs of the decade – the inflatable Blow chair – at the Zanotta company stand in Eurodomus 3, Turin, 1960s.* New techniques combined with a throwaway culture produced many products like this.

**OPPOSITE**

*The Bar in the Spiegel Verlag-shaus, Hamburg, Verner Panton, 1969.* The orange/red colour scheme is lit by the specially designed circular light fittings that were a feature of most of the spaces in the building in various ways.

**ABOVE**

*The staff swimming pool in
the basement of the Spiegel
Verlaghaus, Hamburg, 1969.*

Verner Panton has excelled
himself in this glorious riot
of colour for a space that is
often white and clinical.

**ABOVE**

*Boardroom in the Spiegel
Verlaghaus, Hamburg, 1969. A
quite standard layout for
a Modernist boardroom of
the period has been made
exceptional by the use of
a dramatic single colour
scheme. The chairs are by
Eero Saarinen.*

*The mirrored living room in Tony Duquette's home. This room shows his extraordinary use of found materials and his exotic Baroque approach exemplified in the abalone shell chandelier.*

**LEFT**

*Sitting room by Tony Duquette.*
Duquette was a legendary
Hollywood theatre, film and
interior designer with an eye
for the unusual juxtaposition, over-the-top realization of spaces and uses an
ability to mix and match
the cheap and unexpected
with contrasting objects.

# 1970–1979

In the West, the liberal social values established in the previous decade grew during the seventies. Particularly noticeable was the changing role of women in society and the workplace and the growth of an environmental awareness in some quarters. For industrialized countries, the decade was not always easy: slow economic growth and high unemployment were prevalent, partly due to an oil crisis but also in connection to the volatile markets and a post-industrial reliance on service industries. There also appeared to be an attitude of selfishness and individualism on the rise, rejecting the solidarity of the 1960s. These influences and others resulted in the acceptance of ephemeral and changing lifestyles.

In terms of interior design, there were a number of important developments that reflected the changing nature of the decade. The Modernist approach continued and flourished, particularly in corporate work. A rationalized version of Modernist design that made use of high-technology materials and imagery also began to develop.

### HIGH-TECH

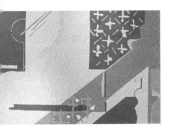

The idea of harnessing new technologies for architecture and interiors have a long history, but those developed by Buckminster Fuller in his Dymaxion houses from 1929 onwards were important: they were all to be made in a factory and then assembled on site, so providing a speedy and efficient autonomous building. A later development in attempts to create economical and speedy production of houses were the California Case Study Houses (1945–66). These adapted Modernist principles and often used industrial materials. A famous example of engineering products used to create a house is the California home of Charles and Ray Eames. However, in this case, the industrial shell held a quite distinctive interior. These earlier expressions of modernity were forerunners of the later High-Tech style.

In contrast to the starkness of many International Style interiors of previous decades, the High-Tech aesthetic of 1970s and 1980s interior design, based on the products intended for industrial use such as heavy-duty flooring, scaffolding and office equipment, introduced its own decorative surfaces and finishes – this approach employed industrial materials in designs that expressed and exposed the technology. A good example of this style is the Hopkins House in Hampstead, London. Built in 1976 and with similarities to the Eames House in Pacific Palisades, California, this steel and glass building, based on a simple structural grid, uses prefabricated industrial materials in an uncompromising way. The irony is that these types of interior often celebrated the industrial through the hand-made or assembled, employing sophisticated joints and expensive materials and finishes.

LEFT
**Michael Hopkins's own house, Hampstead, London, 1976.**
*This house designed for the architect's own use uses a flexible open plan, with Venetian blinds fitted between the internal columns to demarcate the various living functions. The metal decking floor and roof is supported on lattice trusses on freestanding columns. The hi-tech effect is softened by images of domesticity.*

Eva Jiřičná's High-Tech approach, in projects such as Joe's Café and Joseph stores in London, used 'industrial' materials such as aluminium, glass, steel cable and steel tubing. Her engineering background is evident in the interiors she designed. In the 1970s Joseph D'Urso was doing similar things with New York interiors. His own apartment featured mesh grilles as dividers, stainless steel medical sinks and industrial flooring. Although less exciting in terms of interiors, Richard Rogers and Renzo Piano's Pompidou Centre in Paris from 1977 also demonstrated a High-Tech aesthetic, with its clearly defined features relating to the exposed and external building services allowing for large internal exhibition spaces.

**RIGHT**
*Joseph retail store interior by Eva Jiřičná, 1970s.* The high-tech imagery is evident in this view of the purchase point and in the glass stairway.

**BELOW**
*Centre National d'Art et Culture Georges Pompidou, Paris, by Richard Rogers, Renzo Piano, 1971-77.* The 'hi'-tech' transparent tunnels of steel framing and glass that connect the galleries are used for escalators and walkways. They are built on the façade of the building reflecting the design plan of having services on the outside freeing internal spaces.

## MINIMALISM

A different take on the Modernist approach was the development of Minimalism as a style. This method of interior design took the expression 'less is more' to its logical conclusion, with a very limited colour palette and no superfluous furnishings or equipment. The use of simple geometric shapes in as many as possible of the design components defines the style. Minimal colours, defined by textures and simple finishes, are another hallmark.

Minimalism is partly rooted in the simplicity of the Rationalist designers of the early twentieth century. It also connects to ideals of pure form and the fundamental elements of design and space planning. The oft-quoted mantra of Mies van der Rohe, 'less is more', also reflects the aims of the Minimalists, but with close attention to quality and detail.. The work of John Pawson, for example, "focuses on the quality of the spatial sequence and on the refinement of the smallest details of junction, light and surface". During this decade, the Minimalist approach suited a particular type of exclusive retail store, but in domestic interiors it was often softened by textures and interesting shapes.

Pure Minimalism with the imposition of such strict order and regulation, was a limited and specialized taste. For example, in Joseph D'Urso's 1976 apartment for Calvin Klein, the minimalism was seen in the bedroom design, which featured a black leather bed on an island, itself on a platform raised on another platform. The very darkest grey carpeting covered the floor areas and a black rubber-topped table stood at the foot of the bed. The black theme was offset by light walls and ceiling and large windows covered in plain simple drapes.

However, the decade also saw the rise of an important phenomenon in all fields of design that espoused the idea that 'less is a bore'. This new approach was defined as Postmodernism.

## POSTMODERNISM

Postmodern describes a general cultural mood, expressed in such diverse disciplines as literature, philosophy, critical theory, politics, architecture and design. It has also been called New Classicism or Neoclassicism, Pluralism, Eclecticism, Populism, Neo-Rationalism, Romanticism, and New Wave, to name but a few. The underpinning of Postmodernist approaches to design recognizes that life is a problem of organized complexity. This is the opposite approach to the science of simplicity and the concept of a grand narrative which established Modernism.

In 1966, American architect Robert Venturi published his seminal book *Complexity and Contradiction in Architecture*, which effectively gave the Postmodern movement a manifesto. Venturi proposed an architecture and by extension a form of interior design that was all things that Modernism was not, i.e. complex, ambiguous, eclectic, symbolic and historical. The architecture that Venturi produced in the 1960s had close affinities with the contemporary Pop Art movement, and he sought his imagery within mass culture. These buildings' features included an emphasis on content over form, symbolism over rationality and multiple meanings over single meanings.

Postmodernism has a number of common features. First is the recognition of mass culture as a model for design and the consequent blurring of high and low culture: Mickey Mouse can comfortably co-exist with Michelangelo. Second was the continuation of the 1960s concept of the throwaway or expendable: for an increasing number of people, interiors became like fashion – ephemeral and changing. Thirdly, designs were determined by technology and economics rather than any particular concept of form or inbuilt order. In addition, designs were defined by symbols and lifestyles rather than function or morality. Interiors became more multi-functional as old barriers between preconceived room uses and lifestyles were broken down. The rejection of visual purism was a feature which allowed interiors to be designed or decorated with an eclectic assortment of imagery and objects drawn from various cultures and past styles often employing pastiche and parody. Style was often valued over any concept of content as interiors were understood widely as mediums of communication and symbolism, not just as functional spaces.

**BELOW**
*Varna Restaurant, Aarhus, Denmark, by Verner Panton, 1971.*
*This amazing 'pop' interior with its riot of colour, shape and texture is the epitome of Panton's experiments. The foam balls in the ceiling, the chandeliers and the chairs designed by Panton all add up to an extraordinary dining experience.*

**LEFT**
*Mock-up of 'Row house' interior in Renwick Gallery, Washington, by Venturi and Scott Brown, 1976*. This space demonstrates how ordinary homes drew on a range of eclectic sources.

Anti-Design continued the lead set by Archigram, Superstudio and others from the 1960s scene, often using a particular adaptation of popular culture as a source of imagery. Robert Venturi, Denise Scott Brown and Steven Izenour's publication in 1972, *Learning From Las Vegas*, set up a whole new way of looking at culture and encouraged a range of decorating approaches that were eclectic, amusing, challenging, as well as simply colourful and full of imagery.

One interesting example of their approach was the 1976 Renwick Gallery exhibition Signs of Life: symbols in the American city. One of the sections was about the use of signs and symbols in the home through furnishings, decoration, architectural style and details. Mock-ups of suburban interiors showed just how eclectic average American homes could be. A room that had examples of products and designs derived from Regency, Art Deco, Renaissance and Georgian models all in the same space was a clear challenge to architects and designers.

Around the same time but in a different vein, Italian designers were also challenging conventions. The success of The New Domestic Landscape exhibition held in New York in 1972 gave a platform for avant-garde thinking in architecture, interiors and design. A number of small 'room settings' were displayed, which were set up to show both counter-design and pro-design approaches. The counter-design work by Italian companies such as Superstudio and Archizoom emphasized that the world needed social change before physical change. One example was an empty space with just a microphone playing words describing 'destruction' and then countering that with language describing 'utopian imagery'. On the other hand, those that were pro-design considered that improvements in design and interiors would encourage social change. The display of micro-environments by such designers as Ettore Sottsass and Joe Colombo envisaged a new approach to lifestyles that reflected the changing nature of society.

The range and variety of the Postmodern concept can be clearly seen in any comparison. In Verner Panton's 1971 project in Aarhus, Denmark, for the Varna Restaurant, the spaces were decorated in psychedelic colours including bright violet, red, orange and blue in various forms, including in large foam ball shapes. These were in conjunction with his Mira-X fabrics and Panton's own product designs including glass chandeliers and furniture. In stark contrast is the work of Hans Hollein. The latter's Austrian Tourist Office of 1976–78 in Vienna, for example, featured a range of symbols related to exotic travel. These included a railing modelled on an ocean liner, an Indian style gazebo and gilded metal 'palm trees' in a white space, with a ceiling reminiscent of the work of Otto Wagner. This was a fine example of the wit, eclecticism and dual-coding expressed by Postmodern design.

Another of the features of Postmodernism was the use of the historic repertoire, whether from the ancient or the recent past. Carlo Mollino's remodelling of the Teatro Regio in Turin during the 1970s demonstrated this. The auditorium had an oval indigo-coloured proscenium arch, complemented by bright red seats which contrasted with the individual organically shaped cream-coloured boxes. The main space was lit by a huge array of glass 'stalactites' somewhat reminiscent of early Expressionist interiors.

Another use of historic references was the London Biba store. Highly fashionable, with a young clientele, its colour schemes based around blackish-mulberries, blueberries, rusts and plums took inspiration from Art Nouveau, Art Deco and the recent Pop styles.

## OFFICE INTERIORS

Although many office interiors developed along the lines established by the space planners of the 1960s, with open plan offices and sectionalized dividers, a particular manifestation of Postmodern planning and design was the linking of functions with human needs. A fascinating development was the concept of a 'workers' village' developed by the Dutch architect Herman Hertzberger. Hertzberger designed his Centraal Beheer insurance company project, built in 1974 in Apeldoorn, Netherlands, so that the occupants "would have the feeling of being part of a working community without being lost in the crowd." The unfinished concrete building had repeating small platforms, which allowed small groups of people to congregate, and the inhabitants were encouraged to personalize and decorate the space.

New office buildings in the 1970s often still followed the general pattern of narrow runs of cellular offices arranged along a central corridor. The ambition for each employee to work in their own office or among a small group was the new formula that seemed to contradict all the claims of Bürolandschaft. To deal with this, the Swedish design practice Tengbom invented the 'combi-office' idea. This consisted of cellular offices on the exterior of a building, leaving a common space for employees and services in the centre.

**LEFT**
*Interior of Biba store, Kensington, London, c.1971. The orna-mental ceiling and lighting epitomize the fantasy imagery of the store that provided an escapist and al-ternative lifestyle experience for a young generation.*

Another change led by interior design was in the planning of medical facilities. In the 1970s, hospitals began to exchange their sterile, functional image for a friendlier model, to meet the new challenges of the marketplace and to adapt to the changing attitudes to illness and death. The new hospitals, designed to treat patients and families more as guests than as clients, provided public spaces that acted as hotel-like community meeting places and accommodations. These changes attempted to reduce the apparent gulf between patient, community and the hospital experience.

## BRITAIN

In Britain there was a continuation of the mix of common styles, but in the 1970s there were three interesting national trends that were quite different in scope and approach.

The first included the work of designers such as David Hicks. His approach was to use bold colours and patterns, to mix and match antique and modern and large and small scales and to harmonize the architectural spaces with the decoration. His designs were a clever amalgam of the classical tradition and contemporary visualizations. His 1966 drawing room design for Mark Hampton's New York apartment exemplifies this.

The second trend was that of nostalgia: whether it was John Fowler's conservation and re-creation of real country house interiors or the more comfortable but equally prestigious work by firms such as Colefax and Fowler, the taste for English 'country house style' interiors was fuelled by a wistfulness for things past. Designers exported this taste successfully abroad, particularly in the USA, with the work of Mario Buatta among others.

The third trend was towards an alternative to both expensive 'high style' and boring 'high street' products. The Habitat concept, the brainchild of Terence Conran, successfully tapped into a new market demand for alternative lifestyles from the younger generation. Relatively inexpensive, the stores sold an image of an interior part vernacular, part stylish, which allowed consumers to mix and match Scandinavian-influenced pine furniture with brightly coloured patterned textiles and accessories or European bentwood furniture with metal lighting.

## USA

The USA offered a microcosm of 1970s trends. Modernism continued as a design language for many architects and designers. Richard Meier's Douglas House, built between 1971–73 at Harbour Springs, Michigan, is a superb example of a Rationalist house which has clear references to early Modernism and Corbusier. Indeed, Meier furnished the house for his clients with his own furniture products, but also used designs by Le Corbusier and Mies van der Rohe.

A more Postmodern approach was also evident. An example of this was Warren Platner's 1974 American Restaurant in a building for Hallmark Cards in Kansas City. The designer said "it occurred to me that since our client was in the greeting card business, we should treat the space in a very decorative way – like a huge lace Valentine – and everything we did was to enhance that impression." Whether we agree with this or

RIGHT
*Sitting room by David Hicks, 1970s. The trademark 'squared' carpet pattern is the basis for an unusual colour scheme and a mix of modern and traditional objects.*

not, the eclectic mix of bentwood chairs, brass light fittings and the most extraordinary vaulting effects direct from Gothic originals certainly made this a landmark interior.

The continuity of fine decorating was maintained by a number of high-class decorating firms, including Parish Hadley. An example of their work from the 1970s was a commission undertaken by Albert Hadley for the library in the New York apartment of Brooke Astor. The room was an updated classic with an original *rouge royale* fireplace surround, chintz sofas with red flowers and brown stripes and a magnificent collection of leather-bound books fitted into bespoke bookcases complete with brass trims and red lacquered panels. This type of work continued a tradition of society designers where glamour was combined with discipline, quality materials and an eye on the past but still with a sense of the contemporary.

There was also an interest in using references to the vernacular. SOM's work for the Banco de Occidente in Guatemala City (1977–81) used indigenous colours, textures and materials and local concepts such as terraces, fountains, courtyards and trellises, which were incorporated into a Modernist building project. This was a way of linking universal ideas with particular and appropriate regional contexts.

The decade embraced a range of approaches to interiors that framed and responded to the various and eclectic tastes of producers and users. Whether manifestations of Modernism, rooted in historical precedents or reflecting an anti-'good taste' approach, the interiors of the 1970s still reflected the nature of different sectors of society as those of the previous decades had.

*Douglas House, Harbor Springs, Michigan, by Richard Meier, 1973. The four floors of the house mean that circulation is mainly horizontal, with one interior staircase and one exterior, placed so that there is no interruption of the lake views.*

*Banco de Occidente, Guatemala City, by SOM, 1978. The interiors establish links to the particular location through the use of rich colours, textures and materials. The openness of the spaces is expressed through the control of light and shadow.*

**RIGHT**

*The Centraal Beheer office
building, Apeldoorn, by Herman
Hertzberger, 1968–72.*
This office complex consists
of a larger number of equal
spatial units allowing for
maximum flexibility of use.

**ABOVE**
*The Centraal Beheer office building, Apeldoorn, by Herman Hertzberger, 1968–72.* The ground floor showing the open plan layout of the offices.

**ABOVE**

*Brion Cemetery, San Vito d'Altivole, near Treviso in Italy, by Carlo Scarpa, 1969–1978.* The Chapel interior expresses its somber but dignified nature through the rectilinear, and curved sculptural concrete elements that appear to make connections to spirituality.

**OPPOSITE**

*Brion Cemetery, San Vito d'Altivole, near Treviso in Italy, by Carlo Scarpa, 1969–78.* The interior of the chapel showing the formal and symbolic aspects of Scarpa's work.

**OVERLEAF**

*Large lobby of the Hyatt Regency Hotel, San Francisco, by John Portman, 1970.* The enormous atrium associated with Portman's hotel work is evident here as a statement space.

**RIGHT**
*Palladio wallpaper design by Peter Jones, 1971.* The typical blue and purple colourway reflects one of the colour palettes of the period.

**OPPOSITE**
*Palladio wallpaper design by Peter Jones, 1971.* This example demonstrates the imagery of the Art Deco revival.

**ABOVE**
*The Snyderman House, in Fort
Wayne, Indiana, by Michael
Graves, 1972–77.* An unex-
pected mural inside a late-
Modern white house shell.

**ABOVE**
*The Snyderman House in Fort Wayne, Indiana, by Michael Graves, 1972–77.* A fine example of late Modernism, showing the view from the second floor.

**ABOVE**
*Living room in the Mercer House,*
*East Hampton, New York, by*
*Robert A.M. Stern, 1973. The*
*variations on a white*
*scheme comprise a liveable*
*Modernist aesthetic.*

**OPPOSITE**
*Sun room in the Mercer House,*
*East Hampton, New York, by*
*Robert A.M. Stern, 1973. The*
*casual living area with*
*wicker furniture contrasts*
*with a Modernist architec-*
*tural aesthetic.*

**OVERLEAF**
*The auditorium of the Teatro*
*Regio, Turin, by Carlo Mollino,*
*1973. The mass of icicle*
*lights illuminate the red and*
*cream colour scheme.*

**PREVIOUS PAGE**
*Douglas House, Harbor Springs, Michigan, by Richard Meier, 1973*. The amazing lake-view room with chairs by Le Corbusier.

**RIGHT**
*The American Restaurant in Kansas City by Warren Platner, 1974.* The pink and gold scheme with Gothic-inspired vaulting created a fantasy space for dining.

**ABOVE**

*A living room by David Hicks., 1970s.* The coordinated reds of the various elements of the interior create a warm and inviting space that is subtly lit and beautifully accessorized. The contrasting shapes add interest and relieve the dominance of the red colour.

**OVERLEAF**

*Joseph retail store exterior by Eva Jiřičná, 1970s.* This view looking into the shop suggests symmetry in the design planning.

**ABOVE**
*A view of the interior of Michael*
*Hopkins' house, London, 1976.*
*The oriental carpet, soft*
*upholstery and furniture*
*'classics' are in contrast to*
*the high-tech imagery.*

**ABOVE**
*A view of the interior of Michael Hopkins' house, London, 1976.* The use of industrial materials for a Hi-Tech effect is evident in this architect's own home.

**OVERLEAF**
*Interior from the 1970s.* An open-plan space with contemporary artworks, light fitting and an emphasis on natural materials shows one aspect of 1970s taste.

*Mock-up of Row house interior in*
*Renwick Gallery, Washington, by*
*Venturi and Scott Brown, 1976.*
This space demonstrates
how ordinary homes drew
on a range of eclectic
sources.

**ABOVE**
*Mock-up of 'Country house'*
*interior in Renwick Gallery,*
*Washington, by Venturi and*
*Scott Brown, 1976*. *This gallery*
*exhibit combines the idea*
*of 'good taste' (antiques)*
*with modern comfort and*
*function.*

**ABOVE**
*Mock-up of 'Suburban house' interior in Renwick Gallery, Washington, by Venturi and Scott Brown, 1976.* Suburban homes took inspiration from various places.

**OVERLEAF**
*Interior of the Austrian Travel Agency, Vienna, by Hans Hollein, 1976–78.* The references to exotic destinations are evident in this classic Postmodern interior.

**ABOVE**
*Interior view of the Pompidou
Centre, Paris, by Renzo Piano
and Richard Rogers, 1977.* An
industrial-scale interior
showing another version of
the Hi-Tech approach that
was associated with these
architects.

**ABOVE**
*Interior view of gallery arrangement in the Pompidou Centre, Paris, by Renzo Piano and Richard Rogers, 1977.* A combination of traditional gallery spaces within a Hi-Tech envelope.

**ABOVE**
*Sunar Furniture Showroom,*
*Los Angeles, by Michael Graves,*
*1979–80. A detail of the*
*showroom that highlighted*
*the objects in a dramati-*
*cally coloured and lit set*
*of spaces that changed*
*the way showrooms were*
*designed.*

**LEFT**

*Sunar Furniture Showroom, Houston, Texas, by Michael Graves, 1979.* Graves's use of motifs and imagery that were to be stock-in-trade of the Postmodernists is evident here.

**BELOW**

*Sunar Furniture Showroom in New York, by Michael Graves, 1979.* The playful columns, capitals and murals are typical of Postmodern design work.

**ABOVE**
*Banco de Occidente, Guatemala City, by SOM, 1978.* The use of vernacular architectural models of open courtyards, terraces, gardens, fountains and trellises were incorporated into the spaces, that created a contemporary space which related to its locality and clientele.

**ABOVE**
*Banco de Occidente, Guatemala City, by SOM, 1978.* The colour scheme, the rough stucco walls and the local stone flooring reflecting architectural continuity within the building, enhance the serenity of the space.

# 1980-1989

**The 1980s saw many social, political and economic changes that affected interior design. Changing production methods, the internationalization of styles and a more heterogeneous society – as well as growing concerns over issues such as sustainability and conservation – raised many challenges for designers.**

The growth of a worldwide interest in interiors was a manifestation of a certain hedonism, an "anything goes" feeling of living in the moment. Extensive media coverage of interior design fed the demand for details about lifestyles of the rich and famous as well as giving individuals ideas and concepts. Between 1980 and 2005, the number of magazines for interior design grew from 423 to 1,151 worldwide.

Whatever the lifestyle choice, there remained a continuation of the Modernist aesthetic, often in the guise of Minimalism, which offered a form of solace against the world but still imposed a form of regulation on the user. In addition, more rationalised versions of high tech were also found, but many of the major and minor styles and tastes of the 1980s were placed under the umbrella term of Postmodernism and developed from initiatives that originated in the 1970s.

## POSTMODERNISM

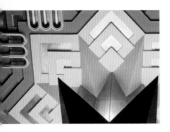

In 1984, Andrea Branzi published *The Hot House: Italian New Wave Design*, which suggested that there was a major change in architecture and design that now looked at design-related issues as well as structural form. Moving away from ideology and style, it considered production and consumption. It was in part a call to reinvent interior decoration and design through the use and application of colour, patterns, crafts skills, material choices and so on. The underpinning idea of Postmodernism recognizes that life is a problem of organized complexity. This is the opposite of the ideal of elegance and simplicity often associated with Modernism.

Postmodernism has a number of identifying features, though it aims to be deliberately challenging and complex. The celebration of 'otherness' and heterogeneity found in society accounts for the pluralist approach to architecture and design since the 1970s. Radical eclecticism, or the mixing of different 'languages' to engage different tastes and cultures and describe different functions, was one of the defining aspects of Postmodern architecture and design.

All of these approaches constitute a return to content and, in many cases, decoration. In addition, they result in a building or object that is not self-referential but reaches out to the rest of us by many associations and references. The furniture of Robert Venturi with historical references to the eighteenth century, Michael Graves using elemental silhouettes of basic forms and interiors and products by the Memphis group demonstrated this critical position,

LEFT
*The First chair by Michele De Lucchi for Memphis, 1983.*
This chair in tubular steel and painted wood panels epitomizes the Postmodern emphasis on design as communication with references to the electronic age.

which recognized pattern and decoration as being acceptable after all. Variations of these approaches during the decade included an appreciation of hedonism and theatricality, new ornamentalism and materiality and a delight in dualism and plurality, as well as interiors that flirted with deconstruction and conceptualism. Into this mix, one can also add ideas such as creative salvage, historical revivals and, significantly, the reuse of older properties that were converted to new uses. These ranged from city-centre lofts to power stations.

## UNITED KINGDOM

In terms of architectural interiors, there were a range of design approaches that reflected a range of contemporary tastes. Versions of Modernism remained popular, particularly with public authority clients. For example, the work by Chamberlin, Powell & Bon for the Barbican Arts Centre in London 1982 is a form of Brutalist-style design with a wide variety of spaces housing several arts venues. A smaller scale example of a sensitive design for an arts museum which took particular heed of its location was Barry Gasson's work for the Burrell Collection in Glasgow which opened in 1983. The design of the building complemented the collection rather than conflicting with it, having dramatic items such as Romanesque doorways built into the structur, while the open glass walls offered views of adjacent grassed areas and woodland.

The taste for varieties of hi-tech Modernism continued. Foster Associates devised a spectacular space designed to sell clothes for the Katharine Hamnett store in London in 1986. There was no recognized shop front; rather a 35-metre bridge of etched glass panels that led into the white open triangular sales area. The 'bridge' was illuminated from underneath to make a dramatic and powerful statement.

At the other extreme was Richard Rogers' Lloyds building in the City of London, completed in 1986. The spectacular interior has the underwriting room on the ground floor, with its breathtaking 60-metre high atrium, lit naturally by sunlight streaming through a vast glass roof. The first four upper levels open onto the atrium space, which is pierced by cross-over escalators that accentuate the middle of the structure and help define the High-Tech nature of the building.

**LEFT**

*Katharine Hamnett Store, London by Foster Associates, 1986.* De-tail of the frontage showing the illuminated bridge into the store.

**BELOW**

*The Atrium of the Lloyds Build-ing, London, by Richard Rogers, 1986.* The view looking up to the barrel-vaulted glass roof showing the hi-tech design features.

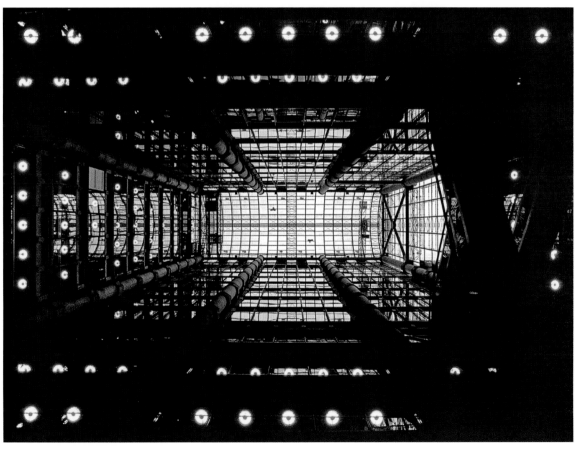

The High-Tech interior continued as a trend for restaurants and bars at this time. Eva Jiřičná's Le Caprice (1981) in London, near The Ritz, and Rick Mather's Zen in Hampstead (1985) offered diners an architect-designed interior to enhance their eating experience. This hedonistic approach was also found in the development of boutique hotels that offered guests a visual experience, rather than just a bed for the night. Anouska Hempel's Blakes Hotel in London was created in 1978 as one of the world's first luxury boutique hotels and was based on her interpretation of Eastern-influenced minimalism.

The Postmodern found its focus in the writings of Charles Jencks. His Thematic House, created in London between 1979 and 1984, was an archetypal set of spaces. Jencks considered that Postmodernism as a movement had lost the true meaning of ornament. He thought that it had collapsed into what he called "kitsch appliqué". Therefore his own house was a testament to his notions of ornament as symbol, where each detail, room and space told a story. His overall theme was time, space and the seasons. Jencks's interiors reflected these concepts through use of focused sets of imagery and stylistic touches.

**BELOW**

*The 'summer room' in the Thematic House, London , by Charles Jencks, 1979–84.* *The yellow colour scheme reflects summer, but the ornament also speaks a Postmodern language of communication and interpretation.*

**LEFT**
*Jigsaw store, Brompton Road
London, by Nigel Coates, 1991.*
*The store offered an anti-
dote to the hi-tech imagery
of the decade with organic
shapes, natural materials
and a narrative approach
to design that makes con-
nections with users.*

Less serious and more playful were the works of architect and designer Nigel
Coates, whose work was eclectic and drew narratives from a wide range of imagery and
materials. His work for the Jigsaw and Katharine Hamnett fashion retailers in London and
Glasgow during the 1980s was designed with his narrative approach clearly visible in
the detailing as well as in the large-scale manipulation of spaces. His designs particularly
attracted attention in Japan. An indication of his approach can be seen in comments
he made about his Caffè Bongo (Tokyo, 1986). He said that it "was an arresting pop-
classical collage. Bursting with vocabulary from the worlds of music and fashion, the
cafe's aircraft-wing-meets-Piranesian-Rome aesthetic expressed the fundamental design
currents of the late twentieth century."

In a different vein, and for a more significant project, was the 1983 Pentagram/Crosby refurbishment of parts of the 1920s Unilever House in London. The use of reinvented Art Deco features, including the zigzag motif, De Stijl derived coloured lights, luxury stone floors and dramatic uplighters, all presented an image of the 1920s skyscraper foyers but in a traditional office block. More overtly Postmodern was Terry Farrell's work for the media company TV-AM in London (1982). This was where Hollywood and Memphis met in a nostalgic exercise in a fun Postmodernist interior design. Columns and ziggurats meet basic over-scaled geometric shapes and mix with Italian Memphis-inspired furnishings, sprinkled with a few High-Tech references for good measure.

## FRANCE

A few well-known names dominated the French approach to the new decorative attitude in interiors in this decade. In fact, the French government officially promoted the Postmodern approach through its commissions to young designers. In 1983, the private apartments of the Élysée Palace were given a revamp, and in 1985, Andrée Putman redesigned the office of the Ministry of Culture. Here she juxtaposed Postmodern furniture with eighteenth-century woodwork to create a lesson in combinations: antique gilding and modern blonde wood furniture working well together.

Philippe Starck's theatrical style allowed him to create interiors that were both image and statement. His trademark spaces were initially restaurants. The Café Costes (1984), with its art historical references and well-known three-legged chair, established his international reputation for interiors and product design. The furniture of Garouste and Bonetti also set challenges to the status quo with many references to the exotic, combined with unusual shapes and unfamiliar materials and combinations. Elisabeth Garouste and Mattia Bonetti's decoration of the Privilege Club Paris created a theatrical and mystical set of spaces using murals, baroque masks and other theatrical motifs. In 1981, they displayed their 'barbarian' iron furniture in the contrasting and traditional venue of established decorators, Gallery Jansen.

**BELOW**

*Institut du Monde Arabe, Paris, by Jean Nouvel, 1987–8. The wall demonstrates the practical and the decorative abilities of traditional latticework widely used in the Middle East to shield the interior from the sun and afford privacy. Here the mechanical, pattern-creating devices filter the light.*

LEFT

**LEFT**
*Gallery in Musée d'Orsay, Paris,*
*by Gae Aulenti, 1986.* *The more*
*traditional gallery space/*
*layout inserted into a*
*disused nineteenth century*
*railway station as a classic*
*example of building re-use.*

A seminal French project of the decade was Gae Aulenti's transition of a disused
railway station into the Musée D'Orsay, Paris, which opened in 1986. Here Postmodern
meets Beaux-Arts in a classic example of adaptive reuse of a cavernous interior space.
Another was Ateliers Jean Nouvel's Institut du Monde Arabe, Paris (1987–88). This fusion
of established Arabic architectural fundamentals with a Modernist design created a
fascinating space that has remained popular. The references to traditional Arab lattice
designs not only reflect the purpose of the building but also allow the modulated light
to act as a modifier of space.

## USA

The USA again saw a wide range of interior design commissions that expressed the heterogeneous nature of the country and its tastes. Whether colonial or country house, Modernist or Minimalist, anything was possible. One approach emphasizes the eclectic nature of the Postmodern. The architects Robert Venturi and Denise Scott Brown described their own house as "a combination of Jugendstil, English Arts and Crafts, and the Continental Art Nouveau", a suitable choice for architects who "like elements that are hybrid rather than pure". Postmodernism could also produce buildings that reflected both humour and contemporary art practices. Frank Gehry collaborated with Claes Oldenburg and Coosje van Bruggen in the design of the Chiat/Day office building in Venice, California. A hugely oversized pair of binoculars stands over the entrance space and within the main body of the cylinders there are small rooms which are lit from above by the 'eyepieces' of the binoculars.

The taste for classic Modernism and Minimalism in the USA was promoted by architects and designers such as I.M. Pei, Richard Meier and Gwathmey Siegel. The work of Vignelli Associates also demonstrated that the original tenets of Modernism were still relevant in the penultimate decade of the century. This did not always mean a clean cut vision of a white cube. Vignelli's work for the Hauserman furniture showroom in Los Angeles,1982, was embellished with fluorescent art work installations by Dan Flavin.

In contrast to this was the work of Emilio Ambasz for the interiors of the Financial Guaranty offices in New York, from 1986. Here they set up screens of double layers of white silk fringe to separate the work spaces, which, in conjunction with overhead lighting, created a calm and ethereal feeling in the spaces.

A continuing taste for flamboyance in restaurant and hotel interiors was also evident in the decade. Sarah Tomerlin Lee's work for the Helmsley Palace Hotel, New York (1977–81), and the Willard Hotel in Washington (1987) demonstrated a particular approach, that of lasting 'good taste', which reflected her role as one-time editor of the magazine *House Beautiful*. Similarly, decorators like Mark Hampton and Mario Buatta continued to decorate the homes of the rich and famous in a sophisticated, elegant and discerning manner.

## OTHER APPROACHES

Although designers had been working around the world for many years, in this decade it became commonplace for Europeans to design for Japan, the Japanese to design projects in the United States and French and Italians to be seen everywhere.

Nigel Coates' work in Japan for hotels and restaurants introduced typically Western iconography into contemporary spaces in major cities. The fact that these were often quite short-lived projects reflects the turnover of fast-but-fashionable design. In a different vein, being slightly less streetwise and jokey, was the work of Philippe Starck. Projects for cafés (Manin, 1987, and Mystique, 1988, in Tokyo), hotels (Royalton, 1989, and Paramount, 1990, both in New York) and boutiques (Hugo Boss, 1991) were soon followed by architectural projects, as well as a continuing interest in furniture and product design.

In this decade Gae Aulenti's work on conversions and building reuse saw the restoration of the Palazzo Grassi as an art museum in Venice, the conversion of an old Italian embassy in Berlin into an Academy of Science and the restoration of an exhibition hall in Barcelona as a museum of Catalan art. Indeed, restoration, conversion and reuse were to be part of the sustainability agenda that really took off in the 1990s.

This decade, with designs ranging from Memphis to Minimalism, was particularly notable for the engagement with decoration and style, whatever the taste. In many cases, design work – whether for retail shops, museum galleries or private houses – often combined approaches such as the use of technology with a particular signature style. It was in this decade that renovations and building reuse also came to the fore and gave prominence to a new interior architecture.

**ABOVE**
*New York Palace Hotel penthouse Triplex Suite with a view of Madison Avenue and the Saint Patrick cathedral, 1990s. The luxury suite has 19 foot (5.8 metre) high floor to ceiling windows and is spread over three floors. An image of luxury remains a feature of hotel interiors.*

**ABOVE**
*Helmsley Palace Hotel by Sarah Tomerlin Lee, 1980.* The first floor overlooking the lobby of the restored New York Villard Mansion.

**LEFT**
*Interior of Frank Gehry's own house, Santa Monica, California, 1980.* The kitchen already shows some interest in Deconstructivist ideas of unusual angles and shapes.

**OVERLEAF**
*The theatre foyer level, Barbican Centre, London, 1982.* The warm orange ceiling acts as a contrast to the Brutalist concrete building shell.

**OPPOSITE**
*Apartment in Trump Tower,
New York, by Gwathmey Siegel,
1983. The apartment boasts
a built in grand piano,
breakfast bar and kitchen in
ash panelling.*

**LEFT**
*TV-am Studios, London, by Terry
Farrell, 1983. A wide range of
Postmodern references to
past styles are included in
this amusing space.*

**LEFT**
*The courtyard of the Burrell Col-
lection, Glasgow, by Barry Gasson, 1983. This space utilizes
the simplicity of natural
materials.*

**RIGHT**
*Foyer of Unilever House, London, by Theo Crosby/Pentagram, 1984.* Detail of column showing reuse of the zig-zag motif derived from Art Deco originals.

**RIGHT**
*Café Costes, Paris, by Philippe Starck, 1984.* The three-legged 'Costes' chair is an icon of chair design.

**OPPOSITE**
*Café Costes, Paris, by Philippe Starck, 1984.* The interior with large Art Deco inspired railway-type clock.

**RIGHT**
*Office of Vignelli Associates,*
*New York, 1985.* A luxurious
interpretation of Modern-
ism as a timeless approach
to interior design.

**ABOVE**
*Lobby of the Willard Hotel, Washington.* Originally a Beaux
Arts design, in 1986 it was
renovated and refurbished
to its former glory.

**OPPOSITE**
*Intimate dining room in the Royalton Hotel, New York, by Philippe Starck, 1986.* The upholstered walls and Starck-designed furniture suggest luxury and exclusiveness.

**ABOVE**
*Lobby of the Royalton Hotel, New York, by Philippe Starck, 1986.* A fine example of using repetition to create an effect that is both functional and decorative.

**RIGHT**
*The Lloyds Building, London, by Richard Rogers, 1986. The first four galleries are connected by escalators through the middle of the building.*

**LEFT**
*The Lloyds Building, London, by Richard Rogers, 1986.* The 60-metre (197 ft) high atrium is lit naturally through a barrel-vaulted glass roof.

**RIGHT**
*Detail of Baroque-influenced windowsill by Nicky Haslam, 1980s. This detail shows how a stylistic approach can be effectively achieved.*

**BELOW**
*Room in the home of Nicky Haslam, 1980s. An example of how a glamorous scheme can be achieved using silver and gilt as the basis for a themed interior space.*

**BELOW**
*Living room by Nicky Haslam,
1980s.* The stylish eclecticism
of a decorator in his own
home.

**OVERLEAF**
*Room in the home of Nicky
Haslam, 1980s.* A cosy,
intimate style is enlivened
by unconventional wall
decoration.

**ABOVE**
*Dining room in Kiltinan Castle, Ireland, by Mark Hampton, 1980s. A splendid but under-stated high-style country-house room setting.*

**OPPOSITE**
*Musée D'Orsay, Paris, interior scheme by Gae Aulenti, 1986. An example of adaptive reuse where the designer creates a unified interior by using a homogeneous stone cover-ing for the floors and walls.*

**OVERLEAF**
*The Laura Ashley look for the 1980s. A room that combined a quintessentially English romantic image with textiles and antique furniture.*

**OPPOSITE**
*'Alice Underground' themed pub/
club by Edmund Smith, Glasgow,
1986. A bizarre Postmodern
approach that sets out to
amuse.*

**LEFT**
*A display of objects in a wall case
by John Stefanidis, 1980s.*

**LEFT**
*Katharine Hamnett store,
London, by Norman Foster,
1986. The refurbishment
of a nineteenth century
warehouse created a retail
space with a minimal but
spacious effect.*

**RIGHT**

*A living space in the Thematic House by Charles Jencks, 1986.* This room shows the combination of eclecticism and symbolism associated with Postmodernism.

**RIGHT**

*L'Institut du Monde Arabe, Paris, by Jean Nouvel, 1987.* The corridor shows the Arab-derived decorative metal sunscreens with active sunlight control..

**OPPOSITE**

*Garey House, Kent, Connecticut, by Gwathmey Siegel, 1986.* The influence of the architectural shell on the interior spaces is evident.

**RIGHT**
*Interior of David Mlinaric's
own apartment, 1980s.* The
'eye' of a successful interior
designer is evident in the
eclectic juxtaposition of
objects.

**RIGHT**
*Interior of David Mlinaric's own
apartment, 1980s*. A passage
where the wall decoration
complements the displays.

**ABOVE**
*Minimalist loft by Moore and Pennoyer, New York, 1988.* De-signed for fashion designer Zoran, this is the ultimate in self-indulgent Minimalism.

**ABOVE**

*The Winter Garden Atrium, New York, by César Pelli, 1988.* A 10-storey glass-vaulted public venue with clear historical and exotic references.

**RIGHT**

*Blakes Hotel, London, by Anouska Hempel, 1988.* A bathroom with a gold and brown scheme that expresses an elegant luxury.

**LEFT**

*Blakes Hotel, London, by Anouska Hempel, 1988. An 'all white room' demonstrating a monochrome approach that is enlivened by textures and shapes.*

**LEFT**

*Blakes Hotel, London, by Anouska Hempel, 1988. A luxuriously elegant table setting.*

**ABOVE**
*Andrée Putman's own apart-
ment in Paris, 1980s. The*
*dining area has an eclectic*
*ensemble of furnishings,*
*including antiques and*
*modern art.*

**ABOVE**

*Andrée Putman's own apartment in Paris, 1980s.* The built-in upholstered bench seating softens the geometry of the architectural shell.

**RIGHT**

*Albert Hadley's own apartment in New York, 1980s.* The surfaces in the elegant alcove are treated in creamy-white with coloured accents.

**OPPOSITE**

*A corner of Albert Hadley's own apartment New York, 1980s.* The vignette of a mirror faced cabinet and tablescape with an old egg box and various decorations is set off by the dramatic red wall covering to create a staged effect.

**OVERLEAF**

*The second-floor sitting room of Andy Warhol's East Side New York townhouse, 1988.* This is a surprisingly eclectic collection of furnishings with no reference to Pop Art.

# 1990-1999

**The last decade of the twentieth century was characterized by a continuing economic prosperity that was mixed with periods of peace and conflicts that destabilized areas of the globe. The realignment of economies after the end of the Cold War created new opportunities around the world. The period was thus a good one for interior design work, as new money joined old to demand ever more exciting public buildings and ever more special private spaces.**

As well as a demand for corporate and healthcare facilities, the demand for hotels, casinos, restaurants and museums provided plenty of work for interior designers. The term 'Interior Architecture' was used to refer to projects associated with adaptive reuse, where an original interior was architecturally altered in addition to being redesigned. High-Tech, Postmodernism, Late Modernism and Deconstructivism were joined by other approaches that were not necessarily exclusive. The issues surrounding and awareness of environmentally friendly design and green buildings, the role and nature of preservation and building reuse and adaptation, the impact of demands for barrier-free and universal design, and increasing East-West crossovers continued to develop. The concept of Chinese feng shui, which relates to positive orientation and layout of buildings, were popularized in parts of the West.

The growth of computing power and software was crucial in meeting the demand of architects and designers, both in matters of concept visualization and detailed working plans. The new media, particularly the Internet, was also a key player in developments during the decade. The broadcasting and publishing media were also responsible for an upsurge in the popularity of interior design as a topic for all. Whether it was the Martha Stewart shows, IKEA's advertising campaign pleas to 'chuck out your chintz', reality television makeover programmes or any of the home magazines that flourished during the decade, there was an enormous interest in interior design and decoration from all groups of people.

### RESIDENTIAL

Interior design of residential properties has been both at the forefront of design practice and, in some cases, remained rooted in tradition. In terms of a small-scale domestic property, for example, the Hauer King House (1994) by Future Systems is a lesson in the application of High-Tech specifications and Minimalist design principles in a London home. The use of steel, aluminium and glass in its overall construction is complemented by white floors, plaster work and metal. This results in flowing sets of spaces, which are illuminated by large expanses of constructional glass. The house is operated by a range of mechanized fittings for shutters, doors and panels.

In some contrast to High-Tech and Modernist new-build concepts was the whole idea of loft living, derived from the reuse of disused spaces. Although not new, it was in the 1990s that the concept came of age. Interior designer Kelly Hoppen's London home, simply called 'The Loft', was a fine conversion of an old school that she redesigned into a fusion of Western ideas, with Eastern objects and a little philosophy thrown into the mix. Hoppen was well known for colour schemes that used neutral fabric shades that contrasted with dark woods to create a very liveable mix that was actually often punctuated with bold coloured accents.

The hybrid loft living of the 1990s was particularly well demonstrated in the Non Kitch Group's work for a loft conversion in Bruges (1995). Here an old factory had its roof partly removed and replaced with glass panels. This lit a large triple-height living area with exposed original wood flooring. The built-in mezzanine floor housed the kitchen and dining spaces, and the sub level had the private areas. While this approach was playful and user-friendly, Claudio Silvestrin's idea of apartment living is nearly as Minimalist as you can imagine. The 300-square-metre Girombelli apartment in Milan, built in 1999, has its space divided between day and night usage by a single 14-metre long frosted glass wall. There is no conventional furniture or fittings and the white stone floor and solar-veiled windows express the designer's desire to create "a place in which to feel serene, still, at peace, free from disorder and vulgarity".

Eva Jiřičná's Prague loft conversion from 1999 comes somewhere in between. She took a 240-square-metre loft space and converted it to have a combination of both the original and the 'inserted' clearly evident. The suspended glass and steel staircase, which is top lit, leads to areas of exposed roof trusses containing modern classic furniture.

**PREVIOUS PAGE**
*Living area of converted Victorian loft, London, by Kelly Hoppen, c.1999. The loft is decorated with neutral taupe colours and bespoke designer furniture.*

**BELOW**
*Girombelli apartment Milan, by Claudio Silvestrin, 1999. The bedroom in this minimalist apartment instills a monastic quality to the space but with subtle overtones of luxury.*

**OPPOSITE**
*Remodelling of a loft in a historic building in Prague by Eva Jiřičná, 1999. This space clearly indicates the original framework and the new inserts.*

Other experiments in architecture and interiors resulted in the organic architectural work of Javier Senosiain in Mexico, where the concept of the interior takes on something of the surreal. In his house called The Shark, located near Mexico City, the interior is a warren of spaces linked by a carpeted corridor tube with furniture built into the walls and floors, giving a sensation of growth from below. A complete opposite is Rem Koolhaas's Villa Dall'Ava, in St Cloud, Paris (1999): an exercise in Modernism with some interesting twists.

In more conventional interiors, colours reflected a natural palette and there was a demand for luxurious-looking and comfortable furnishings, including oversized sofas and chairs and traditional chandeliers. Natural materials were encouraged and leather remained a popular choice for upholstery.

**BELOW**
*'The Shark' building, Vista del Valle, Mexico City, by Javier Senosiain, 1990. The carpeted organic living area with built-in seating.*

**LEFT**
*TBWA Chiat Day office, New York, by Gaetano Pesce, 1995.* *The virtual office doorway demonstrates the idiosyncratic approach to office design.*

## CORPORATE

Although the radical ideas of the virtual office for the1990s did not become ubiquitous, the office environment was softened somewhat, even domesticated in some cases. The Chiat Day offices designed by Gaetano Pesce in New York (1995) tried to offer an alternative office space with no individual workstations, no hierarchy, lots of technology and a vision of team work and play. Though this seemed like a good model it was ultimately unsuccessful partly due to the lack of privacy and personal space.

An example of insertion and adaptive reuse for corporate clients was the project by Erick van Egeraat for the banking firm ING. Their headquarters in Budapest (1992–94) was a renovation of a Neo-Renaissance building. In this case, the designer inserted a two-storied organically-shaped space, used as a boardroom, into the roof of the building. With apparent references to the internal rib cage of a whale, the wooden ribs contrast with the glass elevator and the aluminium Eames chairs. Whether independent and self-sufficient tower blocks, conversions or smaller human scaled garden-based projects, it was clear that some office workers began to enjoy surroundings that were uplifting, engaging and, above all, human-centred.

## RETAIL

New retail interiors proliferated and flourished in the boom economic conditions of the 1990s. The need to differentiate one company's premises from another was evident. Although distinction was a business requirement, many designers often went for a minimal 'museum' look. The differentiation of the interior was what marked out the differing brands. Not surprisingly, fashion houses often led the way.

During the 1990s, John Pawson designed stores for Calvin Klein. These included the flagship store in New York and others in Tokyo and Seoul, all of which have the minimal qualities associated with Pawson's work: grey stone floors, white walls and light effects, all creating a calm and relaxed atmosphere to allow focus on the clothes being sold.

Unlike traditional shops of previous decades, the Helmut Lang flagship fashion store in New York (1997), designed in conjunction with Gluckman Mayner, had the merchandising area placed towards the rear of the shop, freeing the front space for reception. There is a feeling of the gallery about the store: a feature of many top-end brand outlets in the decade. In the landmark store Moss in New York (1994), Harry Allen and Murray Moss further developed the store-as-museum concept that allowed domestic objects to be displayed in glass showcases in all-white spaces, but of course they were all for sale, not just contemplation.

In complete contrast is the McDonald's flagship restaurant in Stockholm (1998) by CKR architects. Here the Scandinavian idiom of blonde woods and a crisp purity is combined with high quality finishes in stainless steel and pine. The whole operation reflects a form of design regionalism that McDonald's encouraged.

**RIGHT**
*McDonald's flagship restaurant Stockholm by CKR architects, 1998. This space demonstrates a local Scandinavian image adapted to a global brand.*

## HOSPITALITY

Another beneficiary of the boom years of the1990s was the hospitality industry. Hotels and restaurants sprang up in response to the demands of travellers, diners and consumers. The whole gamut of styles was used to create fantasy and escapist locations.

Donatella Versace's Palazzo Versace, in Queensland, Australia and designed in 1999 is a luxuriously extravagant hotel that is either loved or hated. The designer imported Italian accessories and materials, and the whole building was furnished with items from the Versace Home Collection which could be ordered from an onsite boutique store, enabling guests to recreate the look and the sumptuousness of the resort boutique in their own homes. In 1991, Julia Monk created a different sort of luxury in the redesign of the St. Regis New York Hotel. The Beaux-Arts building was restored and updated by refurbishing original features such as floors and ceilings but completely reworking guest rooms in a contemporary idiom. This idea of restoration and addition of contemporary features worked well, whether intended as irony or visual fun.

Le Cirque Restaurant in New York, designed by specialist restaurant interior designer Adam Tihany in 1997, also took a listed landmark building, the Villard Mansion, but in this case turned the gilded spaces into a 'circus'. The effect of bright colours, oversized props and lavish and unusual materials all created a very particular dining experience in a Neo-Renaissance building.

**BELOW**
*Palazzo Versace Hotel, Queensland's Gold Coast in Australia, designed in 1999. The lower section of the lobby.*

**ABOVE**

*Sanderson Hotel, London, by Philippe Starck, designed in 1999*. Billiard room showing 1960s stained-glass window by Patrick Reyntiens and John Piper from the original showroom building.

**OPPOSITE**

*Monsoon restaurant, Sapporo, Japan, by Zaha Hadid, 1990*. The restaurant is conceived in two levels. The lower dining area makes reference to ice and the upper relaxation area relates to fire. The sculptural device sometimes called the 'Orange peel' shown here, links the two areas together.

Another example of reuse was Philippe Starck's design work for the Sanderson Hotel, London. Taking a listed 1950s office/showroom building he demonstrated how to ride the Postmodern wave. Starck's particular use of humour and parody mixed the Baroque and contemporary, by putting together the iconic Salvador Dalí's red lips sofa with 1960s mosaics, hand-carved African furniture and Fornasetti-inspired bar stools.

With the rise of globalization and the notion that all city hotel rooms look the same, Toyo Ito's Hotel P, on Hokkaido, was refreshing in that it represented a simpler Japanese aesthetic by avoiding Western furniture and engaging the visitor with simple white rooms that look onto the landscape of Mount Sharidake. Japan is also the home to a very particular design for a restaurant that reflects a local tradition in a cosmopolitan way. Zaha Hadid's Monsoon Restaurant in Sapporo (1990) took its cue from the ice houses of the city. The formal dining area is grey and ice-like with an 'ice' floor; the relaxation area is a complete contrast, with a 'furnace' of yellow, orange and red organic shapes above the sitters.

The luxury London Hempel Hotel (1997), designed by Anouska Hempel, was a small boutique hotel, which took cool white Minimalism to a fine art. Although the individual rooms sported meditation spaces and their own oxygen supply, the taste was probably just too exclusive: the hotel closed in 2012.

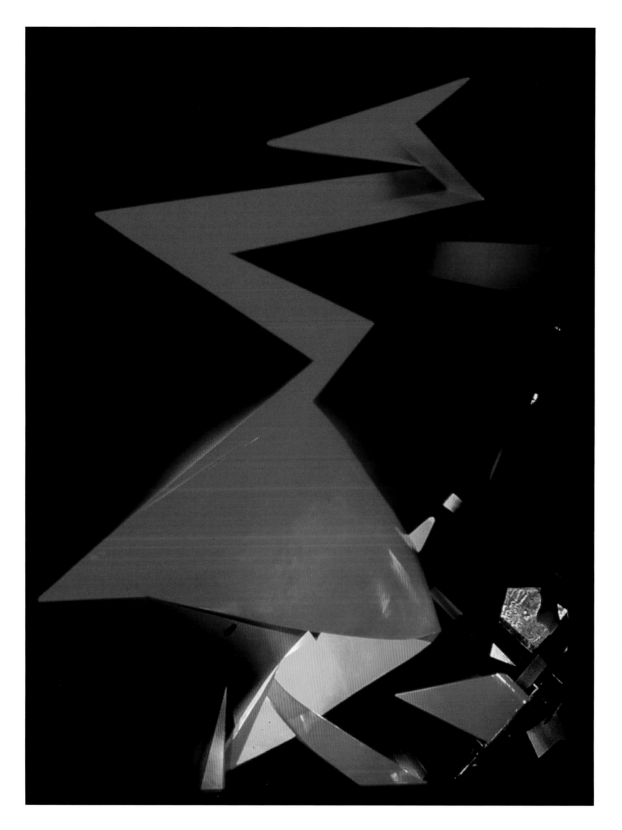

## PUBLIC BUILDINGS

A spate of public buildings created worldwide during the decade produced some interesting interiors. New or refurbished museums were particularly popular. The Groninger Museum in Groningen in the Netherlands, built in1994, was an amalgam of three main pavilions: Philippe Starck's silver cylindrical building, Alessandro Mendini's yellow tower, and an astonishing deconstructivist place by Coop Himmelb(l)au. Being a museum of art, the galleries in each space are artworks in themselves. Mendini's is a closed but colourful space, whereas Coop Himmel(l)bau's is chaotic and open, and both contrast with Philippe Starck's round hall, which is separated by moveable drapes that complement the ceramics displays.

In 1994, Sottsass Associates designed the Museo Del'Arredo Contemporaneo (Museum of Contemporary Furniture) near Ravenna. It is a typical Memphis design approach, using primary colours and geometric shapes to define spaces in a small-scale museum, which has many visually interesting perspectives and patterns that perversely produce an amiable ambience for viewing the displays.

Arguably the most famous museum of the decade was Frank Gehry's Guggenheim Museum in Bilbao. Built in 1997, it is a massive example of Deconstructivist asymmetry, where architecture merges with art in a limestone and titanium masterpiece. Going in a rather opposite direction is the 1994 Minimalist concrete project by Tadao Ando for the Vitra Conference Pavilion in Weil am Rhein, Germany. An essay in concrete, its simplicity is established through a Zen approach that emphasizes the notion of Minimalism, so that the viewer focuses on the feelings created rather than the forms seen.

Postmodernism was still used in public buildings with great success. Will Alsop's Peckham Library in south London, which opened in 1999, used the idea of pods in an enclosed space that would not look like a traditional library. The exterior merged with the interior through a colourful glass façade, while the traditional layout was upturned and elevated so that an open public space was found at entry level, allowing the reading rooms and pods to be above the street level, thus avoiding some noise and nuisance. The idea was to encourage all age groups and ethnicities to use the building and to avoid any connotations of 'libraryness', thus engaging with the public on a popular level both visually and functionally.

At the other end of the scale of learning spaces is John Outram's 1995 reuse of a listed landmark hospital that became the Judge Institute of Business Studies, Cambridge University. The designer's Postmodern additions reflect the power of Classicism but also incorporate the latest technology, creating a set of spaces that are as colourful as they are intellectually challenging. Outram's use of 'floating staircases' and 'seminar balconies' (think of theatre boxes) encouraged interaction, creating a project where the concept of spaces planned for human collaborations is seen at its best.

At the end of the twentieth century, interior designers could look back on a revolutionary set of changes that had been built up over the past 10 decades. The preceding chapters have charted the changes in terms of aesthetics, which have moved with developing and changing tastes and demands. However, perhaps the most dramatic developments have been in other areas. Over the decades, the use of new materials and techniques have brought unprecedented advantages to the designer, changes in the actual practice of interior design and the development of consumer lifestyles and attitudes – whether social, economic or environmental – have all contributed to the growth of a true profession, with the responsibilities and benefits inherent in that status.

**ABOVE**
*Vitra Conference Pavilion, Weil am Rhein, Germany, by Tadao Ando, 1995.* The spaces reflect the use of simple geometric forms, creating a tranquil space.

**RIGHT**
*The 'shark' building, Vista del Valle, Mexico City, by Javier Senosiain, 1990.* The Gaudiesque doorway entrance.

**OPPOSITE**
*The 'shark' building, Vista del Valle, Mexico City, by Javier Senosiain, 1990.* The stairway shows the organic nature of the interior.

**ABOVE**
*Chikatsu-Asuka Historical
Museum, Osaka, by Tadao Ando,
1991–94.* An interior view
that reflects the local kofun
(mounded tombs) in the
surrounding area.

**OPPOSITE**
*Cartier Foundation, Paris, by
Jean Nouvel, 1991–95.* View
of interior glass-and-steel
staircase and street showing the transparency of the
building.

**ABOVE**
*Lee House in Chiba, Japan, by Tadao Ando, 1993.* Living area and detail of courtyard and internal ramp, with traditional Japanese artefacts in a Modernist setting.

**RIGHT**
*Conversion of old stone farmhouse, Provence, by Claudio Silvestrin, 1992.* The bath/shower-room is surfaced in Beauvale stone.

**OPPOSITE**
*Interior of the Cambridge Judge Business School, by John Outram, 1995.* The adaptive reuse of the old Addenbrooke's Hospital in Cambridge.

*Interior of the Cambridge Judge Business School, by John Outram, 1995.* The columns in the galleried walkways demonstrate the use of colour and pattern.

*Interior of the Cambridge Judge Business School, by John Outram, 1995.* Notice the stairways and tiled pillars in particular.

**LEFT**
*Pomerantz apartment, Park Avenue, New York, renovated by Charles Gwathmey, 1995. View of the bedroom showing the featured curved form in the bed alcove.*

**BELOW**
*Pomerantz apartment, Park Avenue, New York, renovated by Charles Gwathmey, 1995. View of the main living area; the fireplace is both a traditional object and a sculptural insertion into the curved wall surface.*

**BELOW**
*Guggenheim Museum Bilbao
by Frank Gehry, 1997. View of
Richard Serra's installa-
tion 'Matter of Time' in the
museum.*

**LEFT**
*Entrance lobby to Guggenheim Museum Bilbao by Frank Gehry, 1997*. A view of the lobby entrance showing the architectural elements within the interior.

**ABOVE**
*Display in The Hempel Hotel, London by Anouska Hempel, 1997. Detail of a simple display and the effects of colour and texture contrasts.*

**RIGHT**
*Bar in Le Cirque restaurant, New York, by Adam Tihany, 1997. An interesting example of an 'insertion' into an existing listed building.*

**OPPOSITE**
*Room in The Hempel Hotel, London, by Anouska Hempel, 1997. The Minimalist Zen influence is evident in this calm space.*

**ABOVE**

*Living space in private apart-
ment, Kensington, London, by
David Chipperfield, 1997–99.*
A Modernist space making
reference to Le Corbusier.

**LEFT**
*Girombelli apartment, Milan, by Claudio Silvestrin, 1999.* The white Minimalist approach enlivened by shapes and textures.

**OVERLEAF**
*Girombelli apartment, Milan, by Claudio Silvestrin, 1999.* The bathroom demonstrates the Minimalist aesthetic with its attention to detail combined with an ethereal effect of light and space.

**LEFT**
*Boardroom in Schroder Bank, London, Gensler, 1990s.* The understated colour scheme and luxury materials reflect a particular corporate image.

**OPPOSITE**
*Corporate office boardroom in London by Gensler, 1990s.* The room is an example of the refurbishment of an interior in a listed historic building.

**ABOVE**
*Hall on 10th floor of Venetian Las Vegas Hotel, 1999. A Venetian fantasy in an escapist location.*

**ABOVE**

*Architect's own home, John Pawson, 1990s. The bathroom with monochrome colour and minimal features create an ascetic experience.*

**OPPOSITE**

*Architect's own home, John Pawson, 1990s. The dining area with built-in storage.*

**RIGHT**
*Architect's own home, John Pawson, 1990s. The kitchen combines a minimal aesthetic with a white decorative scheme.*

**RIGHT**
*Architect's own home, John Pawson, 1990s. The bedroom has built-in storage but with a wood feature in relief.*

**LEFT**
*Architect's own home, John Pawson, 1990s.* The architect's Minimalist aesthetic is evident in the staircase, although moderated by the use of wood.

**RIGHT**

*Pied-à-terre in Athens by John Stefanidis, 1990s.* The wood-lined study reflects a restrained masculine Modernism.

**OPPOSITE**

*Pied-à-terre' in Athens by John Stefanidis, 1990s.* Living space demonstrating how an eclectic approach to furnishing and the value of books are integral to this scheme.

**OPPOSITE**

*Living space in Karim Rashid's New York apartment, 1990s.* Rashid's trademark pink and organic shaped furniture feature here.

**LEFT**

*Kitchen in Karim Rashid's New York apartment, 1990s.* The designer's particular use of pattern and colour is a challenge to the senses.

**OVERLEAF**

*Top of the starircase in the Lowry Centre, Salford, by Michael Wilford, 1997–2000.* The colour scheme reflects the excitement of a theatre space.

**OPPOSITE**
*Sanderson Hotel, London, by Philippe Starck, designed c.1999.* The iconic 'Mae West Lips' sofa creates a feature in the reception.

**LEFT**
*Sanderson Hotel, London, by Philippe Starck, designed c.1999.* The colourful and glamorous Purple Bar.

**OVERLEAF**
*Palazzo Versace Hotel, Queensland's Gold Coast in Australia, designed c.1999.* The dining room with dramatic carpet and centrepiece.

**LEFT**
*Peckham Library by Alsop and Störmer, London, designed c.1999.* The pods in the main library building.

# Index

Page numbers in *italic* type refer to pictures.

Le Caprice restaurant 410

Le Corbusier 20, 74, 122, *122*, *156–7*, 168, *181*, 313, 319, 364

Lee House *468*

Lenygon and Morant 81, 120

Lescaze, William 174

Lessman, Jac *230*

Liberty & Co 28

Liebes, Dorothy *253*

Lissitsky, El 74

Little and Brown 81

Lloyds building 408, *409*, *428–9*

Loewy, Raymond 174, *195*, *249*, *347*

Logan, George *58*

London Transport 170

Loos, Adolf 35, *35*, *69*, *72*, 130

Losch, Tilly 170

Lovell Beach House 128

Lowry Centre *492–3*

Lurçat, Jean 176

Lutyens, Edwin 26

**M**

McClelland, Nancy 81, 128, 130, 175

MacDermott, Beatrice *236*

"machine for living" 122, 168

McKim Mead and White 32

Mackintosh, Charles Rennie 22, 30–1, *31*, 78

MacLachlan, L. *56*

McMillen, Eleanor 128, 175

Maison de Verre 20, 176, *177*, *189*

Maison Jansen *334*

Mallet-Stevens, Robert 123, 130, *137*, *140*, *166*

Malmsten, Carl 78, *328–9*

Mare, André 79, 130, *151*

Margold, J. *160*

Marshall, Hayes *211*

Martin House *62–3*

Martine *146–7*

Marx, Samuel *230*

Masson House 29

Mather, Rick 410

Mathsson, Bruno 221

Maugham, Syrie 24, 169, 176

Mayflower Hotel 220

media influence 15–16

Meier, Richard 364, *367*, *384–5*, 414

Memphis 22, 406–7, *407*, 412, 462

Mendelsohn, Erich 74, 171, *171*, *206*

Mendini, Alessandro 462

Mercer House *380–1*

Mercier Frères *167*

Mewès and Davis 32, *33*, 78

Meyer, Adolf *124*

Mies van der Rohe, Ludwig 20, 22, 24, 34, 126, *126*, 174, *207*, *215*, 216, 319, 359, 364

Miller, Herman 310

Miller, John Duncan *189–90*

Miller House *346*

Minimalism 11, 22, 24, 126, 312, 359, 406, 410, 414, 454, 460, 462

Mink, Valentin *53*

Miró, Joan 214, *216–17*, 218

Miss Cranston's Tea Rooms 31

Mlinaric, David *442*

Modernage Furniture *231*, *234*

Modernism 11–12, 17–22, 34–5, 74, 79, 81–2, 120–8, 168, 170–4, 176, 214, 216, 218, 221–4, *243*, 308, 310, 312–13, 315, 319, 356, 364, 366, 406, 408, 414, 456

*Modernisme* 28

Modulor 20

Mollino, Carlo 223–4, *223*, *240–1*, *256*, 362, *382–3*

Monk, Julia 459

Monsoon Restaurant, Sapporo 460, *461*

Moore and Pennoyer *443*

Morris and Co. *92*, *252*

Morris, William 26, 319

Moscow Underground *232*

Moser, Karl *36*

Moser, Koloman *68*

Moss, Murray 458

Mourgue, Olivier 317

Munthe, Gerhard 78

Musée D'Orsay 413, *413*, *435*

Museo Dell'arredo Contemporaneo, Ravenna 462

Muthesius, Hermann 27, *112–13*

**N**

Nash, Paul 170

National Farmers Bank, Owatonna 34

Neo-Baroque 168

Neo-Classicism 359

Neo-Rationalism 359

Neutra, Richard 215

New Classicism 359

New Wave 359, 406

New York Palace Hotel *415*

Nicholson, Christopher *222*

Niemeyer, Adelbert *91*

Non Kitsch Group 454

# Picture Credits

The publishers would like to thank the following sources for their kind permission to reproduce the pictures in this book.

Key. T: Top, B: bottom, L: Left, R: Right, C: Centre

**Alamy:**
/Julian Castle: 124b, /Bon Appetit: 464b, /Yaacov Dagan: 482 /Elizabeth Whiting & Associates: 363, /Hemis: 415, / Angelo Hornak: 186, /Interfoto: 314, /Patti McConville: 416, /Realy Easy Star/Giuseppe Masc: 460, /V&A Images: 260 (5), 292, 293, /View Pictures: 268

**Arcaid:**
409t, 410, 420, 421t, 422t, 424, 436-437, 439t, 440t, 441, 470t, 474t, 475, 481b, /Rainer Kiedrowski/Bildarchiv-Monheim: 17, /Richard Bryant: 5, 245-247, 370, 371, 426, 427, 455, /John Edward Linden: 263, /Richard Waite: 498-499

**Atelier Hollein**:
/Jerzy Surwillo: 362, 398-399

**© Bjorg Magnea - www.bjorgmagnea.com:**
/View: 471t, 471b

**Bridgeman Art Library:**
34l, /Archives Charmet: 156b, /The Stapleton Collection: 159t

**Centre Pompidou Archive:**
/Archizoom Photo Archive: 309t, 309b, 312, 313

**Claudio Silvestrin:**
468b

**Corbis:**
/Jonathan Bailey/English Heritage/Arcaid: 169, /Morley Von Sternberg/Arcaid: 494, /Alan Weintraub/Arcaid: 260 (4), 299, 304-305, /Bettmann: 334b, /Kevin Fleming: 372-373, /Giuglio Gil/Hemis: 483, /Thomas A. Heinz: 31, /Fernando Bengoechea/Beateworks/Outline: 354, 355,/Kim Kyung-Hoon/Reuters: 343-345, /Ron Sachs/CNP/Sygma: 334t

**© The Courtauld Institute of Art, London:**
232

**The Estate of David Hicks:**
318, 324, 325, 366, 387

**Esto:**
/Jeff Goldberg: 444t

**Fiell Archive:**
10l, 10r, 11, 13, 15, 36, 37t, 37b, 38-39, 40-41, 42, 43, 44, 45, 46, 47, 48, 49, 50-51, 52, 53, 54, 55, 56-57, 58t, 58b, 64, 65, 66-67, 68-69, 70-71, 72tl, 72tr, 83, 84-85, 86-87, 88-89, 90-91, 92-93, 94-85, 96-97, 98-99, 100-101, 102, 103, 104-105, 106-107, 108, 109, 110, 111, 112, 113, 114-115, 116, 117, 118, 119, 121, 122, 132-133, 134-135, 136-137, 138-139, 140t, 140b, 141t, 142-143, 144-145, 146, 147, 148-149, 150-151, 152-153, 154-155, 156t, 157, 158t, 158b, 160-161, 162-163, 164-165, 166, 167, 172, 173, 174r, 178t, 178b, 180t, 180b, 184-185, 188, 189t, 190-191, 192-193, 194, 195b, 198-199, 202-203, 204-205, 206-207, 208-209, 210-211, 217t, 218, 221, 225, 226-227, 228, 229, 230-231, 233, 234-235, 236, 237, 238-239, 240-241, 242, 243, 244, 245, 249, 249, 250-251, 252, 253, 254, 255, 256-257, 258, 259, 260 (1,2,3), 267, 272-273, 274-275, 276-277, 279, 280, 281, 282, 283, 284b, 285t, 285b, 286-287, 288-289, 295, 300-301, 302, 306t, 306bl, 306br, 307t, 310, 316, 320-321, 328-329, 330, 331, 332-333, 335t, 335b, 336-337, 340t, 341, 342-343, 346, 350, 361, 392-393, 407

**Gaetano Pesce:**
/Chiat Day: 457

**Getty Images:**
32, 338, 376, 417, /AFP: 425, 485, /Ernst Haas: 261, /New York Daily News: 450-451, /Time & Life Pictures: 216, 278, 307, /José Fuste Raga: 60-61, /UIG/View: 472

**Glasgow Museums Collection:**
421b

**© Helene Binet:**
476

**Interior Archive:**
443b, 446, 447, /Tim Bedow: 484, 485, 486, 487t, 487b, /Mark Luscombe-Whyte: 446, 447, 448, 449, /Simon Upton: 490, 491, /Fritz von der Schulenburg: 430t, 434, 442t, 442b, 444b, 445b, 488, 489

**iStockphoto.com:**
29, 30l, 30r

**Javier Senosiain:**
456, 464, 465

**Library of Congress, Prints and Photographs Division:**
27, 62, 63, 72b, 73, 80t, 80b, 174l, 175, 200, 290-291, 294, 311

**Lindmanphotography.com:**
/Åke E:son Lindman: 458

**Mary Evans Picture Library:**
/Goran Algard/IBL: 284t, /CCI/Epic: 296b, /PVDE/Epic: 303, /Interfoto: 348, /National Magazine Company: 296b, 297t, 297b, 339, /Retrograph Collection: 349

**Matthew Weinreb:**
390

**Michael Graves & Associates:**
378, 379, 402, 403t, 403b

**Montreal Museum of Fine Arts:**
/Christine Guest: 223

**National Trust:**
212

**Nigel Coates Studio:**
411

**Otto Archive:**
367t

**Palazzo Versace:**
459, 496-497

**Peter Moore and Peter Pennoyer:**
/Reto Halme: 443

**Photo12:**
/Archives du 7e Art/MGM: 317

**RIBA Library Photographs Collection:**
213, 222, /Architectural Press Archive: 298, /Roland Halbe: 59b, /Alistair Hunter: 438,  /Joe Low: 391, /John Maltby: 9, 340b,  /Paolo Rosselli: 201, /Edwin Smith: 34,

**Scala Archives:**
/Museum of Modern Art, NY: 217

**Sotheby's:**
127

**Skidmore, Owings & Merrill:**
© Nick Wheeler: 367b, 404, 405

**Tadao Ando Architects & Associates:**
/Mitsuo Matsuoka: 467, 468t,

**Topfoto.co.uk:**
/IMAGNO/Austrian Archives: 59t

**V&A Images:**
374, 375, /Raymond Loewy™ is a trademark of Loewy Design LLC, licensed by CMG Worldwide. www.RaymondLoewy.com: 347

**Venturi Scott Brown:**
394-395, 396, 397

**Verner Panton Design:**
351, 352, 353, 360, 377

**View Pictures:**
412, 439b, /Ethel Buisson/Artedia: 326-327, /Michel Denance/Artedia: 358b, 400, 401, /Stephane Couturier/Artedia: 413, 422b, 423, 435, /Zooey Braun/Artur: 463, /Tomas Reihle/Artur: 409b, 429, /Peter Cook: 358t, 388-389, 428, 469, 470b, 492-493, /Chris Gascoigne: 481t, /Dennis Gilbert: 408, 466, 473, /Hufton + Crow: 480, /James Morris: 454, 475, 478-479, /Danica O. Kus: 418-419, 440b, /Ronald Tilleman: 365, 368, 369, /Andreas Von Einsiedel: 453

**Wiki Commons:**
8, 20, 21, 25, 33, 35t, 35b, 75, 76, 77, 133, 124t, 125, 126, 128, 131, 141b, 159b, 171, 177, 179, 181, 182-183, 187, 189b, 195t, 219, 264, 269, 270, 315t, 315b

**Yale University Library, Manuscripts & Archives:**
386

**Zaha Hadid:**
/Paul Warchol: 461

Every effort has been made to acknowledge correctly and contact the source and/or copyright holder of each picture and Carlton Books Limited apologises for any unintentional errors or omissions, which will be corrected in future editions of this book.

# Bibliography

Adamson G & Pavitt, J. (eds) *Postmodernism: Style and Subversion, 1970-90,* London V & A Publications. 2011.

Banham, J., (ed), *Encyclopaedia of Interior Design*, 2 Vols, Chicago & London: Fitzroy Dearborn, 1997.

Benton T., and Sharpe, D., *Form and Function: a Source Book for the History of Architecture and Design 1890-1939,* London: Granada Publishing, 1975.

Benton, T. *Art Deco 1910-1939,* London, V& A Publications, 2003.

Calloway, S., *Twentieth Century Decoration*, London: Weidenfeld and Nicolson, 1988.

Duncan, A, *Art Deco Complete: The Definitive Guide to the Decorative Arts of the 1920s and 1930s* , London, Thmes and Hudson, 2009.

Edwards. C. *Interior Design  A Critical Introduction*, London,  Berg, 2011

Fahr-Becker, G. *Art Nouveau*, Ullman 2011.

Harrison-Moore, A. and Rowe, D.C., (eds.), *Architecture and Design in Europe and America 1750-2000*, Oxford: Blackwell, 2006.

Heinz, T, *The Vision of Frank Lloyd Wright*, Edison, Chartwell, 2003.

Jackson, L. *Art Deco Complete: The Definitive Guide to the Decorative Arts of the 1920s and 1930s*, London, Phaidon,1988

Leslie, F. *Designs for 20$^{th}$ century interors*, V & A Publications, London, 2000.

Pile. J., *A History of Interior Design*, London: Laurence King, 2006.

Sparke, P., *Elsie De Wolfe: the Birth of Modern Interior Decoration*, New York: Acanthus Press, 2005..

Tate, A. and Smith, R., *Interior Design in the 20$^{th}$ century*, New York: Harper and Row, 1986.

Taylor, M. (ed.) *Interior Design and Architecture: Critical and Primary Sources*, Berg, London, 2013.

Venturi, R., *Complexity and Contradiction in Architecture*, New York: The Museum of Modern Art, 1966..

Wharton, E., and Codman, O., *The Decoration of Houses*, London: Batsford, 1898.

Wilk, C. *Modernism: Designing a New World : 1914-1939*, London, V & A Publicaiton, 2008

Wolfe, E. de, *The House in Good Taste,* New York: Century, 1914.

# Acknowledgements

I would like to thank Peter and Charlotte Fiell for first suggesting the idea behind this book and for commissioning me to write it. At Carlton Books, Isabel Wilkinson has been an excellent editor for the project and I thank her for successfully seeing it through the publishing processes. In addition, her picture research colleagues have done sterling work in locating the many and varied images found in the book, for which I thank them. Finally, I thank my wife, Lynne Edwards, for her caring and constant support and her consistent interest in and encouragement of my work.